NASTY NEIGHBOURS

by Debbie Isitt

WARNER CHAPPELL PLAYS

LONDON

A Warner Music Group Company

NASTY NEIGHBOURS
First published in 1995
by Warner Chappell Plays Ltd
129 Park Street, London W1Y 3FA

ISBN 0 85676 213 X

AMATEUR PRODUCTIONS
Royalties are due at least fourteen days prior to the first performance. A royalty
quotation will be issued upon receipt of the following details:

Name of Licensee
Play Title
Place of Performance
Dates and Number of Performances
Audience Capacity
Ticket Prices

PROFESSIONAL PRODUCTIONS
All enquiries regarding professional rights (other than first class rights) should be
addressed to Warner Chappell Plays Ltd, 129 Park Street, London W1Y 3FA. Enquiries
regarding all other rights should be addresed to A P Watt Ltd, 20 John Street, London
WC1N 2DR.

OVERSEAS PRODUCTIONS
Applications for productions overseas should be addressed to our local authorized
agents. Further details are listed in our catalogue of plays, published every two years,
or available from Warner Chappell Plays at the address above.

Printed by Commercial Colour Press, London E7

FOREWORD

During my research for NASTY NEIGHBOURS I discovered that many of us have difficulties living "next door" to people at some stage in our lives and I wanted to explore why that should be so. Could it be a lack of community spirit? Should we all be throwing street parties and leaving our front doors open like they did in the good old bad old days? Or could it be that we've lost (if we ever had it) the ability to communicate with each other? And if we have, then it wouldn't just be with people we barely know like new neighbours, but with our families, our partners, even ourselves? And if a lack of real communication causes conflict then it would be little wonder that there was so much conflict. I began to recognise that in a society that values property so highly, that it invests more in bricks and mortar than in people, the concept of *nasty* neighbours could be deemed an inevitable outcome rather than a spot of bad luck. If we are all so inadequate at understanding each other, then what else is there to do but call anyone who is not us "them" and build a moat around our castles and arm ourselves with weapons and engage in wars that none of us can win. And what really struck me about all this was that at the end of the day most of us don't even own our own castles and they can be snatched away from us at any minute. We live in fear — fear of each other, fear of failing and fear of losing our security and with it our sanity/reality and that's why it's really difficult to live next door to each other.

There is a real sense of urgency in these characters — of time running out — and their absolute terror is a shrewd starting point for motive. They are not caricatures, but real people — I know — I've met them. And through meeting "them", I have realised that I am not alone.

I would like to thank the actors who worked on various stages of development for this play: Mark Kilmurry, Lucy Richardson, Morgan Edwards, Nick Whitfield and Mike Dwerryhouse, their talented participation in script workshops, rehearsed readings, etc, was invaluable. Thanks to Gary Tanner for his patient listening and encouraging feedback. Thank you also to Marilyn and Paul Hodge for their generous contribution to the research process.

Debbie Isitt
1995

NASTY NEIGHBOURS was commissioned by British Telecom for the 1995 BT Biennial in association with the Little Theatre Guild of Great Britain, and was premiered in October/November, 1995 by the following theatres:

Abbey Theatre Club, Arbroath
Chenderit School, Banbury
CB Drama Group, Belfast
Bingley Little Theatre, Bingley
Crescent Theatre, Birmingham
Festival Players, Bollington, Macclesfield
Little Theatre, Bolton
Phoenix Theatre Company, Bolton
Bradford Playhouse, Bradford
Brampton Park Theatre Company, Brampton
New Venture Theatre, Brighton
Miller Centre, Caterham
Green Room Club, Carlisle
CHADS, Cheadle Hulme
Chorley Little Theatre, Chorley
Colchester Theatre Group, Colchester
Pickwick Theatre Company, Corsham
Criterion Theatre, Coventry
Marlowe Players, Derby
Guild of Players, Dumfries
Dunstable Rep Theatre, Dunstable
Colne Valley Theatre Group, Earls Colne
Nomads, East Horsley
Exeter Little Theatre Company, Exeter
Felixstowe ADOS, Felixstowe
Formby Theatre Club, Formby
Troupers Theatre Company, Frome
Gainsborough Theatre Company, Gainsborough
Gosforth ADS, Gosforth
Caxton Players, Great Grimsby
Halifax Thespians, Halifax
Hall Green Little Theatre, Birmingham
Hayling Island ADS

Heald Green Theatre Company
Archway Theatre, Horley
Hyde Little Theatre, Hyde
RAF, High Wycombe
Holywood Players, Holywood, Eire
Ilkley Players, Ilkley
Priory Theatre, Kenilworth
Nonentities, Kidderminster
Grand Theatre, Lancaster
Loft Theatre, Leamington Spa
Lancastria Theatre, RAF Waddington, Lincoln
Questors Theatre, Ealing, London
South London Theatre Centre, London
Venturers Drama Group, London
Macclesfield ADS, Macclesfield
Mossley AODS, Mossley
GTC at Barton Green, New Malden
New Forest Players, New Milton
NOMADS, Newmarket
Dolman Theatre, Newport, Gwent
Apollo Theatre, Newport, IOW
Lacemarket Theatre, Nottingham
Oldbury Rep Theatre, Oldbury
Penrith Players, Penrith
Prestwich ADOS, Prestwich
Progress Theatre, Reading
Richmond Shakespeare Society, Richmond
Strand Theatre Company, Rochdale
Romsey AODS, Romsey
Rugby Theatre, Rugby
Company of Ten, St Albans
SPADES, Salford
Studio Theatre, Salisbury

Sawston Players, Sawston
Shaftesbury Arts Centre, Shaftesbury
Sharnbrook Mill Theatre Trust, Sharnbrook
Shawbury Players, Shawbury
Dilys Guite Players, Sheffield
Shoreham Village Players, Shoreham
Westovian Theatre Society, South Shields
Southport Dramatic Club, Southport
Lytton Players, Stevenage
Stockport Garrick Theatre, Stockport
Royalty Theatre, Sunderland
Highbury Players, Sutton Coldfield
Tavonians, Tavistock
Toddington ADS, Toddington
Tonbridge Theatre and Arts Club, Tonbridge
Wellington Civic Players, Taunton
Lindsey Rural Players, Wickenby
Wilstead Players, Wilstead
Chesil Theatre, Winchester
Wokingham Theatre, Wokingham
Woodley Theatre, Reading
Sharon Players, Tel Aviv

CAST OF CHARACTERS

The action takes place in the Peach's and the Chapman's adjoining houses, and at the Hodge's home in Australia.

The time is the present.

ACT ONE

Scene One

Loud Latin music by the "Gipsy Kings" fills the stage during the blackout. Lights come up on MR PEACH *in his living room. It is evening. He is on the telephone, music fades out as he speaks.*

MR PEACH Hello? Hello? Hel . . . yes, I'm still here . . . oh, thank you. Come on . . . come on . . . hurry up, you stupid . . . hello! Hello! Hello! HELLO . . . Oh, yes please — of course I'll hold, you turd . . . come on . . . come on . . . what are you doing? . . . Just put me through, pick up the phone and SPEAK TO ME!!! One . . . two . . . three . . . four . . . five . . . six elephants . . . seven elephants . . . eight elephants . . . nine elephants . . . FUCKING SPEAK TO ME!

     (*He hangs up as* MRS PEACH *enters. She moves quietly to the window.*)

MRS PEACH I hope they keep their nets clean.

MR PEACH Why shouldn't they?

MRS PEACH Susan kept hers spotless.

MR PEACH I know.

MRS PEACH Spotless she was . . .

MR PEACH Meticulous she was . . .

MRS PEACH I hope they don't have small children.

MR PEACH They won't.

MRS PEACH How do you know?

MR PEACH It's not big enough, is it?

MRS PEACH   Dogs, they might have dogs.

MR PEACH   I hope they don't have dogs.

MRS PEACH   A cat would be alright.

MR PEACH   You say that now.

MRS PEACH   I wonder what he does?

MR PEACH   What does he drive?

MRS PEACH   It's red.

MR PEACH   Is it?

MRS PEACH   Deep red.

MR PEACH   Burgundy?

MRS PEACH   No, definitely not burgundy, more red than that.

MR PEACH   Not bright red?

MRS PEACH   No, not bright red, dark red.

MR PEACH   Oh dark red.

MRS PEACH   With an alarm.

MR PEACH   Oh yes? I doubt they'll have dogs then.

MRS PEACH   Do you?

MR PEACH   Very much.

MRS PEACH   As long as they keep clean nets.

MR PEACH   And windows.

MRS PEACH   Well that goes without saying.

MR PEACH   But will it?

MRS PEACH   Yes, I should think so.

MR PEACH   You look nice.

MRS PEACH	Do I?
MR PEACH	That colour suits you ever so much.
MRS PEACH	Does it?
MR PEACH	Yes!
MRS PEACH	I wasn't sure.
MR PEACH	Oh, ever so much.
MRS PEACH	How was it today?
MR PEACH	Good. It was good today. Bitterly cold but productive.
MRS PEACH	You made a sale then?
MR PEACH	No, but something very interesting happened. I was walking past this woman wearing a woolly hat and scarf when her hat suddenly flew off in the wind, it was so fierce that the hat blew straight off. And it came to me, had that woman had her hat somehow attached to the scarf it wouldn't have flown into the road and then she wouldn't have had to leave the pushchair on the pavement and nearly kill herself trying to retrieve the hat.
MRS PEACH	Go on.
MR PEACH	I don't know why no one has thought of it before. The all-in-one hat and scarf, there's a mint in that.
MRS PEACH	Maybe they already sell them — maybe they're just not popular.
MR PEACH	You know what I mean do you? A scarf that is knitted into a hat — I don't mean tied on with bits of string.
MRS PEACH	Yes, I think so.

Mr Peach	Well I don't know anywhere that sells them. Do you?
Mrs Peach	Not off the top of my head, Harold.
Mr Peach	Oh — you made a little joke there, Jean — top of my head — hat and scarf — do you get that?
Mrs Peach	Yes, I think so.
Mr Peach	I'm going to look into it — could make us a mint.
Mrs Peach	What happened to her?
Mr Peach	Who?
Mrs Peach	The woman with the baby?
Mr Peach	Well I don't know. I'd walked past her, hadn't I?
Mrs Peach	Didn't you make sure she was alright?
Mr Peach	Of course she was alright, Jean — I was just telling you about her to make the point about the design idea.
Mrs Peach	I know you were Harold, but you said she was in the middle of the road trying to get her hat back and the baby was on the pavement.
Mr Peach	I said the pushchair was on the pavement, not the baby.
Mrs Peach	Yes, but the baby was in the pushchair, wasn't it?
Mr Peach	I don't know — it could have been empty.
Mrs Peach	Women don't push empty pushchairs around, Harold.
Mr Peach	I just think you're missing the point, that's all.

(*Slight pause.*)

MRS PEACH	What will David Withers say?
MR PEACH	About what?
MRS PEACH	About you not making a sale.
MR PEACH	He only said to me yesterday — Peach, we're lucky to have you on the team.
MRS PEACH	Did he?
MR PEACH	He did.
MRS PEACH	Well he is, he is lucky to have you on the team.
MR PEACH	I know, that's why he said it.
	(*Slight pause.*)
MRS PEACH	Have you done the pools coupon?
MR PEACH	Yep. It's all ready.
MRS PEACH	He's usually been by now.
MR PEACH	Do you fancy a sherry?
MRS PEACH	Yes, alright.
MR PEACH	And some music? How about your Latin favourite?
MRS PEACH	Yes, go on then.
MR PEACH	We could even have a twirl.
MRS PEACH	Not tonight — I'm a bit tired.
MR PEACH	No? Alright then.
	(*Latin music is playing softly.* MR PEACH *and* MRS PEACH *sip their sherry.*)
MR PEACH	I'm going to order you a new rug.
MRS PEACH	What?
MR PEACH	In that colour.

MRS PEACH	What colour?
MR PEACH	The exact same colour as you are wearing. That colour suits you.
MRS PEACH	Don't you like this rug then?
MR PEACH	It's nice but it doesn't match your skin tone so well as the new one will.
MRS PEACH	I'll have to re-coordinate the soft furnishings if you change the rug.
MR PEACH	Will you?
MRS PEACH	It might even mean new wall coverings.
MR PEACH	But you might find it works as is.
MRS PEACH	There's a strong possibility that it won't.
MR PEACH	Well you're in charge of that department, Jean.
MRS PEACH	When?
MR PEACH	I'll get it delivered in a few days.
MRS PEACH	Will you bring me a sample?
MR PEACH	No, it'll be a surprise.
MRS PEACH	What are we going to do with this one?
MR PEACH	There's nothing wrong with it.
MRS PEACH	So what shall we do?
MR PEACH	Sun roof?
MRS PEACH	Pardon?
MR PEACH	Did it have a sun roof, his car?
MRS PEACH	Yes I think so.
MR PEACH	Throw it away.

MRS PEACH	I could put it in the spare room.
MR PEACH	Throw it away.

(*Slight pause.*)

MRS PEACH	What time is it?
MR PEACH	Eight thirty-five.
MRS PEACH	They're going out, look . . .
MR PEACH	Both of them?
MRS PEACH	Yes, come and have a look, turn the lamp off.

(MR PEACH *and* MRS PEACH *turn the lamp off and peer out of the window.*)

Can you see them?

MR PEACH	It's a bit dark.
MRS PEACH	She's looking over.
MR PEACH	Don't wave!
MRS PEACH	She can't see me anyway, there wouldn't be any point.
MR PEACH	He can't find his keys.
MRS PEACH	Ah, bless him.
MR PEACH	Found them!
BOTH	Top pocket!
MRS PEACH	She's not dressed up very warm.
MR PEACH	Well they're probably off to some dinner and dance affair.
MRS PEACH	Still, need a coat — it's freezing — look at the frost on the windscreen.

(*They move away and put the lamp back on.*)

We should really have popped round and
introduced ourselves.

MR PEACH   There's plenty of time, let them settle in.

MRS PEACH   They might have needed something.

MR PEACH   Cup of sugar?

MRS PEACH   You know what I mean, we could have offered
                them a cup of tea, they might not have
                anything in. That's probably why they've gone
                out, because they've got no water on or food
                in.

MR PEACH   They would have let us know if that was the case.

MRS PEACH   They might be shy. It's our responsibility to
                offer.

MR PEACH   Well I'll tell you what, first thing in the
                morning I'll pop my head round, shall I? Just
                in case.

MRS PEACH   Yes, I think so.

MR PEACH   Right you are then.

MRS PEACH   Another sherry?

MR PEACH   I don't see why not. Did anyone ring today?

MRS PEACH   Were you expecting a call?

MR PEACH   No, I just wondered if anyone rang.

MRS PEACH   No, no one.

                (*A beat.*)

MR PEACH   The pools man must have given up tonight.

MRS PEACH   Too cold probably.

MR PEACH   Still, it wouldn't stop me.

MRS PEACH	Maybe you should sell him one of your hat and scarves in one — keep him going.
MR PEACH	Do I detect a hint of sarcasm there, Jean?
MRS PEACH	No I mean it, he could be chasing his hat down the street right at this very moment.

(MR PEACH *looks at his wife suspiciously*.)

MR PEACH	I wonder what time they'll be back then?
MRS PEACH	Funny thing to do on your first night in your new home isn't it?
MR PEACH	Do you remember our first night here?
MRS PEACH	Of course I do.
MR PEACH	We were so excited. An empty house and we thought it was a palace. It's come on a bit since then, eh Jean?
MRS PEACH	We've had some good times in this house Harold, very good times.
MR PEACH	Now don't you get snivelling.
MRS PEACH	I'm not . . . it's just so different without them.
MR PEACH	You couldn't wait to get rid of them!
MRS PEACH	Not the kids! Susan and Jim.
MR PEACH	Imagine Jean, it's summer there now, they'll be doing the old barbie on the beach.
MRS PEACH	It's morning there now.
MR PEACH	I know what — let's give them a ring, eh? Surprise them!
MRS PEACH	No Harold, it's too expensive.
MR PEACH	Rubbish! Come on — lets do it!
MRS PEACH	They might still be in bed.

MR PEACH	Well it's time they were up then — don't want them to miss any of that sunshine do we?
MRS PEACH	Go on then.
	(MR PEACH *rings the number and they both huddle around the phone.*)
MR PEACH	It's engaged.
	(*Disappointed, he replaces the receiver and they sit down.*)
MRS PEACH	I wonder who they're talking to then.
MR PEACH	I don't know. Maybe they left the phone off the hook by mistake. No, I know who it is — it'll be him phoning his boy — he can phone him whenever he likes now he only lives round the corner.
MRS PEACH	Oh, yes.
MR PEACH	We'll try again in a minute.
MRS PEACH	No, another time maybe.
MR PEACH	Shall I put the telly on?
MRS PEACH	No.
MR PEACH	Game of Scrabble?
MRS PEACH	I don't like Scrabble.
MR PEACH	That's because you always lose.
MRS PEACH	That's because you always cheat.
MR PEACH	I Spy, then?
MRS PEACH	No, Harold.
MR PEACH	What then?
MRS PEACH	Pass me my Littlewood's book.

(*He does.*)

MR PEACH   How were the little buggers today?

MRS PEACH   Alright.

MR PEACH   No riots then?

MRS PEACH   Not today.

MR PEACH   Eat up all their greens, did they?

MRS PEACH   They don't look like they've got any kids then, do they?

MR PEACH   Well they're not going to take kids to a dinner and dance affair.

MRS PEACH   Well, what have they done with them, then — left them on their own in the house?

MR PEACH   No, they didn't look the type.

MRS PEACH   Do you like these cushions?

MR PEACH   Let's see . . . oh yes, very Laura Ashley, very smart!

(*She begins filling in order forms.*)

I might as well turn in then.

MRS PEACH   I'll be up in a minute.

MR PEACH   You stay where you are, enjoy yourself!

MRS PEACH   I won't be long.

(*He moves into the bedroom as she fills out catalogue forms. The music builds as he takes a stack of bills out of a hiding place and begins doing some sums. As* MR PEACH *lies down on the bed,* MR CHAPMAN *sits up in bed on the other side. The Latin music disappears and classical music takes over.*)

Scene Two

The lights have changed to the Chapman's. MR CHAPMAN
squints. It is morning. ELLEN, *his wife, has classical music
playing and she is banging nails into a wall in order to hang
a picture.*

MR CHAPMAN   Ellen! . . . Ellen! . . . ELLEN!

MRS CHAPMAN   WHAT!?

                  (*He gets out of bed and joins her in the sitting
                  room.*)

MR CHAPMAN   What are you doing?

MRS CHAPMAN   What does it look like?

MR CHAPMAN   Here, I'll do it.

MRS CHAPMAN   I'm perfectly capable of knocking a few nails
                  into a wall, Robert.

MR CHAPMAN   It's seven o' clock!

MRS CHAPMAN   Is it really?

MR CHAPMAN   Do you have to do that now?

MRS CHAPMAN   Yes.

MR CHAPMAN   I've got a headache.

MRS CHAPMAN   Then you've only got yourself to blame.

MR CHAPMAN   That banging is giving me a headache!

MRS CHAPMAN   The scotch is giving you a headache, the
                  scotch that is flowing through your system!

MR CHAPMAN   Stop banging!

MRS CHAPMAN   No!

                  (*He grabs the hammer off her.*)

You know you really shouldn't drink, Robert
— you obviously can't take it!

MR CHAPMAN   I can take it very well.

MRS CHAPMAN   Can you?

MR CHAPMAN   If this is about last night . . .

MRS CHAPMAN   What about last night?

MR CHAPMAN   It's normal you know, when you're tired.

MRS CHAPMAN   Don't tell me what is normal, Robert!

MR CHAPMAN   I'm exhausted!

MRS CHAPMAN   There's always an excuse.

MR CHAPMAN   You didn't exactly help.

MRS CHAPMAN   Oh well, if its help you need I can book you in
somewhere, there are clinics for men with
your problem.

MR CHAPMAN   I haven't got a problem!

MRS CHAPMAN   Just face it Robert — you made a mistake.

MR CHAPMAN   What are you talking about?

MRS CHAPMAN   You don't fancy me.

MR CHAPMAN   Please God, not again!

MRS CHAPMAN   Well if it wasn't the drink, it must be me.

MR CHAPMAN   Alright it's you! Is that want you want to
hear?! I HAVE got a problem, a problem with
you and drink and sex and nails being
knocked in the wall at seven o' clock in the
morning!!!

MRS CHAPMAN   There's no need to shout, Robert. I'm not
living in a dump.

Mr Chapman	This is not a dump!
Mr Chapman	Isn't it? Then what is it?
Mr Chapman	It's our new home!
Mrs Chapman	Our wonderful, semi-wemi, pre-war new dump.
Mr Chapman	I need a coffee.
Mrs Chapman	There isn't any.
Mr Chapman	I'll go out and get some then, shall I?
Mrs Chapman	Shall you?
Mr Chapman	Do you want anything?
Mrs Chapman	Coffee won't cure a hangover.
Mr Chapman	Do you want anything?!
Mrs Chapman	No.
Mr Chapman	Right!

(*He is about to leave when she picks up the hammer again and resumes banging.*)

	Why don't you start unpacking the boxes instead?
Mrs Chapman	Oh I quite like it like this, don't you? Boxes in a box.
Mr Chapman	This is not a box! It is a very nice house.
Mrs Chapman	A very what house?
Mr Chapman	We can do a lot with it.
Mrs Chapman	Like what?
Mr Chapman	We can restore it properly.
Mrs Chapman	To its former grotesqueness!

MR CHAPMAN	You liked it yesterday!
MRS CHAPMAN	Well I don't like it today!
MR CHAPMAN	You're not giving it a chance!
MRS CHAPMAN	I thought you'd gone to get coffee?
MR CHAPMAN	I have!

(*He slams out. She hangs her Salvador Dali and stands back.*)

MRS CHAPMAN	Christ, what a dump!

(*The classical music fades out with the lights.*)

Scene Three

Lights change to the Peach's. MR PEACH *stands at the window.*

MR PEACH	It was him, he's slammed out the front door, he looks a right misery.
MRS PEACH	I thought he looked nice last night.
MR PEACH	It was dark then, Jean.
MRS PEACH	Is he off to work already?
MR PEACH	He hasn't gone to the car, he's walked past it . . . he's walking down the road.
MRS PEACH	Where's he going then?
MR PEACH	Maybe he walks to work, maybe he works around here.
MRS PEACH	Around here? Doing what?
MR PEACH	He might work at a shop.
MRS PEACH	Not with that car, Harold.

MR PEACH	It might not even be his car — it might be hired.
MRS PEACH	It might be hers.
MR PEACH	I had planned to pop round there this morning.
MRS PEACH	I don't know if you should after all that banging.
MR PEACH	Well they've got to settle in Jean, they've probably got a lot to do.
MRS PEACH	Jim left that house in perfect condition.
MR PEACH	I don't know Jean, he could be a bit slack in the DIY department.
MRS PEACH	Rubbish, he was a perfectionist, they both were.
MR PEACH	Don't you remember that time the handle fell off the back door?
MRS PEACH	Oh you're always bringing up that handle. Once it fell off — once in sixteen years '— and he screwed it back on there and then, and it only fell off because you jerked it so hard!
MR PEACH	I did not jerk it hard — I hardly touched it! All I'm saying is there could be other slack fittings, doors could be falling off hinges, paper could be peeling off walls, shelves could be slipping from brackets —
MRS PEACH	You're making it up!
MR PEACH	Will you tell me what they were banging for at seven o' clock in the morning unless that place is a death trap!?
MRS PEACH	That house was and is the most beautifully maintained house in the Close!

MR PEACH	Not counting ours, Jean.
MRS PEACH	Yes counting ours — it's fantastic!
MR PEACH	Well if it's so fantastic why didn't we buy it off them?
MRS PEACH	I wanted to.
MR PEACH	When?
MRS PEACH	When it was up for sale — I wanted to buy it off them.
MR PEACH	But it's exactly the same as ours!
MRS PEACH	It had nicer things.
MR PEACH	It did not!
MRS PEACH	It did, it had that Italian dining furniture.
MR PEACH	That's got nothing to do with the house! Furniture isn't fixtures and fittings, you don't buy furniture with the house Jean, they shipped that to Australia!
MRS PEACH	I knew that.
MR PEACH	Well if it's Italian dining furniture you want why don't you say? You can have it, I'll buy it for you!
MRS PEACH	When?
MR PEACH	When?! Whenever! Next week!!
MRS PEACH	Boiled egg or muesli?
MR PEACH	Boiled egg.
MRS PEACH	Toast or buttered bread?
MR PEACH	Buttered bread.
MRS PEACH	Tea or coffee?

MR PEACH	Pot of tea.
MRS PEACH	Right.

(*She moves off into the kitchen to put the kettle on.* MR PEACH *peers out of the window.*)

MR PEACH	He's back, look . . . he's coming down the street. He's got something in his hand . . . I can't really see . . . yes I can! Newspaper and a carrier bag. HE'S BEEN DOWN THE SHOP, JEAN! He looks freezing.

(*She reappears.*)

MRS PEACH	Ah, bless him.
MR PEACH	What about me? Out there in all hours, I am.
MRS PEACH	I bless you, too.
MR PEACH	Do you?
MRS PEACH	Course I do.
MR PEACH	I'll tell you what he could do with this morning . . .
MRS PEACH	What?
MR PEACH	A two-in-one hat and scarf.
MRS PEACH	He seemed very nice, actually.
MR PEACH	Who?
MRS PEACH	Him, next door.
MR PEACH	When did he seem very nice?
MRS PEACH	Yesterday.
MR PEACH	You saw him yesterday?
MRS PEACH	Yes.
MR PEACH	To speak to?

MRS PEACH	Yes Harold, he doesn't bite you know.
MR PEACH	WHEN did you speak to him?
MRS PEACH	When you were in the bath.
MR PEACH	You spoke to HIM when I was in the bath?!
MRS PEACH	Well not when I was in the bath, Harold.
MR PEACH	You never said.
MRS PEACH	He's very very nice. In business, he is.
MR PEACH	That's what he said, is it? He's in business?
MRS PEACH	More or less.
MR PEACH	Oh, very dodgy.
MRS PEACH	What do you mean?
MR PEACH	What's he got to hide then?
MRS PEACH	Absolutely nothing, he was very nicely spoken.
MR PEACH	They're the worst.
MRS PEACH	Why are they?
MR PEACH	You can be very naive, Jean.
MRS PEACH	Why have you always got to try and spoil everything? You're jealous, that's all.
MR PEACH	Rubbish!
MRS PEACH	You are jealous because I spoke to him first.
MR PEACH	Rubbish, utter rubbish!

(*Short pause.*)

We'll have our breakfast and then I might pop round there.

Scene Four

MR CHAPMAN has just entered with his carrier bag. He looks at the hung painting.

MR CHAPMAN   That looks nice.

MRS CHAPMAN   Is nice a word you've taken to using since we
                  moved to Net City? Did you bump into Mr and
                  Mrs Nice at the corner shop when buying your
                  nice biscuits to dunk in your nice cup of tea?

MR CHAPMAN   Would you like one?

MRS CHAPMAN   I'll have coffee, black, no sugar.

MR CHAPMAN   Please.

MRS CHAPMAN   Please and thank you, how nice.

                  (*She moves to the window.*)

                  Oh my God, have you seen this?!

MR CHAPMAN   What?

MRS CHAPMAN   This Godforsaken thing parked out here, why
                  do they build houses without garages?

MR CHAPMAN   Huh?

MRS CHAPMAN   Never mind. I'll offer them a sheet to throw
                  over it. How was it out there?

MR CHAPMAN   Cold.

MRS CHAPMAN   Lots of twitching nets?

MR CHAPMAN   No.

MRS CHAPMAN   I'm taking these down.

MR CHAPMAN   I thought you valued your privacy?

MRS CHAPMAN   We can put up some blinds.

MR CHAPMAN   Fine.

MRS CHAPMAN   Oh come on, Robert!

MR CHAPMAN   What?

MRS CHAPMAN   Help me out here.

MR CHAPMAN   What do you want me to do?

MRS CHAPMAN   Anything, something.

MR CHAPMAN   Do you mean with the house?

MRS CHAPMAN   I don't know what I mean! There doesn't seem
                  to be any point!

MR CHAPMAN   To what?

MRS CHAPMAN   To us.

MR CHAPMAN   Ellen, don't . . .

MRS CHAPMAN   I'm not. I can't do this!

MR CHAPMAN   You're stressed out.

MRS CHAPMAN   I'm not stressed out, I'm bored!

MR CHAPMAN   How can you be bored? You said yourself
                  there's a lot to do.

MRS CHAPMAN   You shouldn't have brought me here.

MRS CHAPMAN   It was the best I could do.

MRS CHAPMAN   You didn't try hard enough!

MR CHAPMAN   It was the best I could do! Ask the estate
                  agent, there was nothing on the market —
                  people are sitting on their nests at the moment
                  and that's all there is to it.

MRS CHAPMAN   We could have moved anywhere — anywhere
                  in the world — South America, Africa,
                  Iceland, India — but you brought me here and
                  I don't know why — there must have been a

point! I've lived everywhere there is to live in
this pissy little country — towns, villages,
cities and now a cul-de-sac! A fucking cul-de-
sac!! A wonder of the western world, the
shape of it the curve of the road, the dead end!
This is where people come to die, Robert!!
This is where they come when they've given
up the fight! Yesterday I imagined I was
floating above it and when I looked down all I
saw was teeny-weeny little people going about
their business — little people with balding
heads and winter jumpers mowing lawns and
painting fences and pruning hedges and
rushing about, in and out with nodding heads
and forced smiles going about their teeny-
weeny little business and I suddenly got this
tremendous urge to piss on them and so I did,
I pissed on them from a great height and do
you know what they did? They put up their
umbrellas!!

MR CHAPMAN   You're not doing yourself any good you know.

MRS CHAPMAN   Aren't I?

MR CHAPMAN   You will make yourself ill.

MRS CHAPMAN   No I won't, its YOU I'll make ill — YOU who
can't SEE!

MR CHAPMAN   I can see perfectly well.

                  (*She starts ripping the net curtains from the
                  window.*)

                  Shall I help you take them down?

MRS CHAPMAN   You never take them down any more.

MR CHAPMAN   If you want me to take them down now, I'll
take them down now.

MRS CHAPMAN   I'm not talking about the nets.

MR CHAPMAN   Don't be childish.

MRS CHAPMAN   Come here.

MR CHAPMAN   What for?

MRS CHAPMAN   Come here!

(*He moves to her, tentatively. She kisses him.*)

Go on Robert, take them down.

Scene Five

MR PEACH *is dressed in his suit and tie.* MRS PEACH *prepares to hand over his accessories.*

MR PEACH   Brief case?

MRS PEACH   Check.

MR PEACH   Umbrella?

MRS PEACH   Check.

MR PEACH   Gloves?

MRS PEACH   Check.

MR PEACH   Car keys?

MRS PEACH   Check mate.

(*She throws his keys to him.*)

Do you think the car will start this morning?

MR PEACH   I should think so.

MRS PEACH   Only it's raining.

MR PEACH   Is it?

MRS PEACH   Cats and dogs.

MR PEACH   Mice and men!

Mrs Peach	You haven't got time for that Harold, if you're going to call next door.
Mr Peach	Right you are then. I won't be long.
Mrs Peach	Send them my regards.
Mr Peach	I will!
	(*He goes to leave.*)
	Jean?
Mrs Peach	Yes?
Mr Peach	Do I look alright?
Mrs Peach	Very smart, very classy.
Mr Peach	First impressions and all that.
Mrs Peach	You look super-duper!
Mr Peach	Right.
	(*He exits.*)

Scene Six

Mrs Chapman *is trying to make love to* Mr Chapman *when the door bell rings.* Mr Chapman *looks relieved.*

Mr Chapman	There's someone at the door!
	(*He jumps up and starts doing his trousers up.*)
Mrs Chapman	Charming darling, really charming.
Mr Chapman	Anyway, I'm late.
Mrs Chapman	Run then darling, off you squeak.
Mr Chapman	Why do you always do this to me?
Mrs Chapman	What?
Mr Chapman	And answer the door, can't you?

MRS CHAPMAN   No!

MR CHAPMAN   Great! Really great Ellen, thanks a lot!

(He answers the door.)

MRS CHAPMAN   Who was it?

MR CHAPMAN   No one there — must have imagined it.

MRS CHAPMAN   Of course you didn't imagine it, I heard it myself!

MR CHAPMAN   Well there wasn't anyone.

MRS CHAPMAN   Well isn't that a coincidence?

MR CHAPMAN   What's that supposed to mean?

MRS CHAPMAN   You are always saved by the bell!

MR CHAPMAN   Like I said, I'm late for work.

MRS CHAPMAN   Don't keep your master waiting, run along like a good slave.

MR CHAPMAN   I'll be back by six.

MRS CHAPMAN   Why? Is there a cul-de-sac curfew that I am unaware of?

MR CHAPMAN   Alright then I won't be back by six — expect me when you see me.

MRS CHAPMAN   I take it that means drunk?

MR CHAPMAN   Take it whichever way you like.

(He goes to leave.)

MRS CHAPMAN   Oh, Robert?

MR CHAPMAN   What?

MRS CHAPMAN   Have a "nice" day!

(*He slams out. She picks up an ashtray and hurls it across the room where it smashes as it hits the front door.*)

Scene Seven

MRS PEACH *is in her raincoat, ready to go to work.* MR PEACH *has recently returned from next door.*

MR PEACH	There were some funny noises coming from round there . . . I think one of them was being sick.
MRS PEACH	Being sick?
MR PEACH	I got to the door and I could hear vomiting so I rang the bell but no one came.
MRS PEACH	Well you can't expect them to come if one of them is vomiting.
MR PEACH	Well, no.
MRS PEACH	I wonder what caused that then?
MR PEACH	Maybe they had prawns last night at the dinner and dance.
MRS PEACH	You don't think they had one drink too many?
MR PEACH	Well, they drove home.
MRS PEACH	Must have been the prawns then.
MR PEACH	They might be alright in a few minutes, I'll give it 'til twenty past and pop round again.
MRS PEACH	Another pot of tea then?
MR PEACH	Might as well.

(MRS PEACH *goes to make the tea.* MR PEACH *pulls an envelope out of his inside pocket and secretively reads the letter within.*)

Scene Eight

Aborigine music fills the stage as the lights fade up on the Hodges. They sit on a balcony overlooking the action. They are in Australia and are dressed in matching dressing gowns. It is a hot night.

MRS HODGE   Get me another one will you?

MR HODGE   Sure.

MRS HODGE   What time is it?

MR HODGE   Eight fifty-five.

MRS HODGE   Another five minutes, then.

MR HODGE   Now don't get fretting.

MRS HODGE   (*reading*) England is always beautiful this time of year, hope you're not missing it too much. The move-in was quick, a couple of weeks and the place should be furnished. Don't know if it will be to your taste but will send you photos if we get a chance.

             (*She puts the card down.*)

             That'll be nice, won't it?

MR HODGE   Can't wait.

MRS HODGE   Neither can I.

MR HODGE   Lets have a look at it.

             (*She flicks the card across to him.*)

             That's their garden, is it?

MRS HODGE   Looks like it.

MR HODGE   So they've made this themselves then?

MRS HODGE   Looks like it.

Mr Hodge	Should go into business, English garden postcards could make them a mint!
Mrs Hodge	I must suggest that when they ring!
Mr Hodge	Only another three minutes.
Mrs Hodge	Can't wait!
Mr Hodge	Neither can I.
Mrs Hodge	Didn't you have a drink?
Mr Hodge	No, didn't fancy one.
Mrs Hodge	Is it your stomach?
Mr Hodge	It's a bit queasy.
Mrs Hodge	You want to see a doctor.
Mr Hodge	It's alright, I'll be alright.

(*The telephone rings.*)

Mrs Hodge	Don't answer it. Not if you're feeling queasy.

(*They let it ring. It does not stop.*)

Scene Nine

Mr Peach *is on the telephone speaking in a hushed tone.*

Mr Peach	Come on, come on. ANSWER. Are you deaf? Is your end NOT ringing out? Are you OUT? Answer the phone, pick up the phone, oh stick it up your arse! Hello? Sorry . . . eh yes, the name is Peach . . . eh yes . . . ref 5434612F, thank you — idiot! Yes? It's about this letter you've sent me, that's right, well it's not possible — we have a gas fire and cooker, you see. Oh, I had no idea. Well, well, what to do? I can't. There is none. I'll have to go now.

(*He hangs up quickly as* Mrs Peach *enters.*)

MRS PEACH	Who was that, Harold?
MR PEACH	David Withers.
MRS PEACH	Oh yes?
MR PEACH	I was letting him know that I might be a bit late this morning.
MRS PEACH	What did you tell him?
MR PEACH	I told him you weren't feeling very well.
MRS PEACH	Why did you say that?
MR PEACH	Because I can't tell him that I'm waiting for the neighbours to stop throwing up, can I? I said you had the flu.
MRS PEACH	Well shall I be feeling better soon Harold, only I've got to go in myself shortly?
MR PEACH	Yes yes, I'll pop round again now, shall I?
MRS PEACH	Drink your tea, now I've made it.
	(*He takes his tea over to the window.*)
MR PEACH	I don't believe it!
MRS PEACH	What?
MR PEACH	His car's gone!
MRS PEACH	Stolen?
MR PEACH	No Jean, they must have gone to work.
MRS PEACH	Ah, never mind.
MR PEACH	Glad they're feeling better.
MRS PEACH	You're sure it was vomiting are you?
MR PEACH	Pretty sure.
MRS PEACH	What if it wasn't?

MR PEACH	Well it's none of our business.
MRS PEACH	That's no attitude — what if they've been robbed and murdered in their beds? What if that vomiting was really them being bludgeoned to death?
MR PEACH	At nine o' clock on a Thursday morning?
MRS PEACH	You don't think murderers work weekday mornings, then?
MR PEACH	I don't think they do Jean actually, no.
MRS PEACH	Alright then, what if it was her being murdered by him?
MR PEACH	And why would he want to do that on his first day in their new home?
MRS PEACH	It's very traumatic moving house, that's when all of these domestic murders happen.
MR PEACH	Oh, I thought they happened when the wife made the husband late for work by talking rubbish.
MRS PEACH	Have it your own way.
MR PEACH	Come on.
MRS PEACH	You've left a letter there — look, on the sofa.
MR PEACH	I'll get it!
MRS PEACH	Don't forget the brolly as well. It's tipping down out there.
MR PEACH	Right you are.

Scene Ten

MRS CHAPMAN *is taking her nets down from the window. She spots them next door.*

MRS CHAPMAN   (*to herself*) Here we go, Mr and Mrs Net-Twitch. Come on, have a good look. Don't pretend to point at your flower bed, look straight in. That's it whisper in her ear, usher her to your wreck like she's a cripple, open her door . . . that's the way, now one more look over. Go on wave, I dare you to — oh surprise, surprise, you haven't got the bottle. Tootle-pip!

(*She swings around.*)

Oh hell, what a nightmare!

(*The telephone rings. She answers it.*)

Hello, Ellen Chapman. No he isn't. Who's calling please? Hello?

(*She lights a cigarette.*)

Damn!

Scene eleven

MR PEACH *is in a spotlight centre stage, facing the audience. He has his briefcase at his feet and a clipboard and pen in hand. He speaks to customers.*

MR PEACH   Morning Madam, or is it Miss? I wonder if you can spare me a few moments of your time to help me with a national survey — it won't take long.

(*The sound of the door shutting in his face is loud and clear — Bang!*)

Morning Madam, or is it Miss? I wonder if you can spare me a few moments of your time to help with a national survey? I promise you it won't take long. Thank you very much indeed Madam. Have your windows been

replaced in the last five years? Thank you. Do
you have double glazing? On all windows?
OK. Was the company who carried out the
work any of these four? Staybrite, RSV
Windows, Glazing Mate or Pierce Ltd? I see.
And how much did it cost? I don't know
Madam, its market research . . .

(*Bang!*)

Thank you! Morning Madam, or is it Sir?

(*Bang!*)

Good morning is your Mother in? Hello
Madam, he's a lovely little chap, isn't he? I'm
calling on behalf of National Window
Research plc regarding double glazing. I
wonder if you could spare me a couple of
minutes of your time to answer a few simple
questions? It really won't take long — just two
minutes!

(*Bang!*)

THANK YOU SO MUCH! Good morning Sir,
I've just been examining the state of your
windows, I've been sent to the area by Market
Forces plc to inspect windows and offer an
obligation-free introductory chat — can you
spare a few moments? Well they're in a
terrible state, Sir. HAVE YOU EVER
THOUGHT OF CLEANING THEM?!!

(*BANG! BANG! BANG!*)

Scene Twelve

*Latin music and moody lighting mark the time shift to early
evening at the Peach's house.* MRS PEACH *is looking out
through a crack in the net curtain. She appears nervous. She
is pacing around anxiously when* MR PEACH *enters from work.
She runs straight to him.*

MRS PEACH	There were men. Two men. They came to the door.
MR PEACH	Who were they?
MRS PEACH	They followed me from school — off the bus — they followed me. Two of them!
MR PEACH	What did they want?
MRS PEACH	I don't know — I got inside and ran upstairs. They knocked on the door but I didn't answer!
MR PEACH	Two of them you say?
MRS PEACH	Two of them — both men!
MR PEACH	I wonder who they were?
MRS PEACH	They were shouting!
MR PEACH	What did they shout?
MRS PEACH	I couldn't hear. I put the shower on.
MR PEACH	You had a shower?
MRS PEACH	Yes. I didn't know what else to do!
MR PEACH	Well they've gone now.
MRS PEACH	Strange though, wasn't it?
MR PEACH	Very strange.
MRS PEACH	Do you think they'll come back?
MR PEACH	No, shouldn't think so.
MRS PEACH	Good. I didn't like them. I was looking at the tiles — when I was in the shower. They could do with a change, I don't like them any more. I think they should be white.
MR PEACH	Oh yes?
MRS PEACH	Kind of Victorian.

MR PEACH	Yes that should look very nice. Did anyone see these man follow you to the door?
MRS PEACH	I don't know, I don't think so.
MR PEACH	Good, Victorian, excellent.

Scene Thirteen

It is the same evening. The Chapmans are at home.

MRS CHAPMAN	I am asking you a simple enough question. Did you hand out this phone number to anyone?
MR CHAPMAN	No!
MRS CHAPMAN	You're lying!
MR CHAPMAN	Don't do that! Don't do that "you're lying" thing. I said No. No! No! No!
MRS CHAPMAN	I hate you!
MR CHAPMAN	You don't even know who it was — it could have been anyone!
MRS CHAPMAN	It wasn't anyone — it was your ex-wife!
MR CHAPMAN	Well I don't know how she got the number!
MRS CHAPMAN	Did you ask for ex-directory?
MR CHAPMAN	Yes, maybe they put us in the book by mistake — how do I know?
MRS CHAPMAN	Because you do know! I know you know.
MR CHAPMAN	Oh I forgot — you know everything!
	(*They fume for a moment in silence.*)
	Look forget it. It won't happen again.

MRS CHAPMAN   You promised me she wouldn't call here!

MR CHAPMAN   It won't happen again, Ellen. Look, look at
               the candlesticks, please. They'll look great in
               the study.

MRS CHAPMAN   What study?

MR CHAPMAN   I thought we could turn the box room into a
               study. You can do all your research in there,
               put up your couch, make it comfortable for
               your clients.

MRS CHAPMAN   Fuck you, Robert.

MR CHAPMAN   What? We can throw the carpet out and expose
               the floorboards, it'll look professional.

MRS CHAPMAN   Shut up, will you?

MR CHAPMAN   You've got to try and imagine it, Ellen.

MRS CHAPMAN   You know what I want that box room for, you
               know damn well what that box room is for.

MR CHAPMAN   You need a study.

MRS CHAPMAN   Don't tell me what I need.

MR CHAPMAN   There isn't room in this house Ellen. It isn't
               the right time. We talked about it, you agreed.

MRS CHAPMAN   I did not!

MR CHAPMAN   Well I seem to remember you wanting a study
               in the last seven houses, in fact not having a
               study seemed to make life very difficult!

MRS CHAPMAN   That was then.

MR CHAPMAN   You've got your final exam in three months
               time. You'll be practising by Easter. It's what
               you've worked for, why throw it away?

MRS CHAPMAN   I am NOT throwing it away.

MR CHAPMAN   I think you are.

MRS CHAPMAN   Well when the hell did you start thinking?
                How dare you imagine that you can influence
                my choices!

MR CHAPMAN   Ellen I'm your husband.

MRS CHAPMAN   So what?

                (*Short pause.*)

MR CHAPMAN   I need a drink.

MRS CHAPMAN   Sure you do!

MR CHAPMAN   I've had a pisser of a day at work. I don't need
                this!

MRS CHAPMAN   Then tell me what I am supposed to do?
                Explain to me how I am supposed to handle
                this!

MR CHAPMAN   You're the expert!

MRS CHAPMAN   Then in my expert opinion you have a problem
                that you cannot face up to and you won't let
                me help you and that leaves me nowhere and
                you don't seem to give a shit.

MR CHAPMAN   What an interesting diagnosis.

MRS CHAPMAN   I want one, Robert!

MR CHAPMAN   It's not that simple!

MRS CHAPMAN   How simple can it be? You load it, you aim it
                and you fire it — God knows I'll be doing all
                the complicated bits.

MR CHAPMAN   I'm not ready.

MRS CHAPMAN   You don't have to be!

MR CHAPMAN   Yes I do!

MRS CHAPMAN   Did you have any biology lessons at school?

MR CHAPMAN   Of course.

MRS CHAPMAN   Did you pay attention?

MR CHAPMAN   Yes!

MRS CHAPMAN   Did they tell you that the female clock goes
                    tick-tock, tick-tock and the alarm bell starts
                    sounding in her head as soon as she hits thirty
                    and that the bell will deafen her with its
                    warning and keep her from sleeping and
                    working and living and no matter how much
                    her so called partner keeps trying to find the
                    button that stops the bell there is no let-up, it
                    just keeps ringing louder and louder even
                    when he hits her over the head with his
                    hammering protests, did they tell you that
                    Robert? Huh?

MR CHAPMAN   Did they tell you?

MRS CHAPMAN   No — damn it. They didn't tell me either.

MR CHAPMAN   We've still got time, Ellen.

MRS CHAPMAN   Oh, but the bells Robert, the bells.

MR CHAPMAN   You need to relax.

MRS CHAPMAN   It's so claustrophobic here. We should have
                    moved near the sea.

MR CHAPMAN   Go with it Ellen, stop fighting this place.

MRS CHAPMAN   If you stop fighting you die.

MR CHAPMAN   If you stop fighting you live.

MRS CHAPMAN   Well then. I think we have a difference of
                    opinion.

MR CHAPMAN   Can't you play it my way for a little while?

MRS CHAPMAN   It's not your way though is it? The rules are
                    already made up, the winner has already been

                    chosen and you still imagine you stick a
                    chance.

MR CHAPMAN   I'm just optimistic, that's all.

MRS CHAPMAN   And does the future look bright from the
                    bottom of your whisky bottle?

MR CHAPMAN   Brighter than yours, I think.

MRS CHAPMAN   There you go again — thinking.

MR CHAPMAN   I'll try not to.

MRS CHAPMAN   Good, it doesn't suit you.

                    (*He pours himself another drink.*)

                    I saw our new neighbours today — Mr and
                    Mrs Net-Twitch. They were looking into our
                    house.

MR CHAPMAN   Well what do you expect? I'd have a sly look
                    in their house if they had nothing at the
                    windows!

MRS CHAPMAN   You're as sad as they are then.

MR CHAPMAN   It's not sad to be curious about the people who
                    have just moved next to you, the people who'll
                    be living along side you.

MRS CHAPMAN   Come on Robert, they're nosy old gits!

MR CHAPMAN   Don't be so horrible, you don't even know
                    them.

MRS CHAPMAN   Oh I know them alright!

MR CHAPMAN   You really must stop this knowing everything.

MRS CHAPMAN   Why, does it make you feel inferior?

MR CHAPMAN   Did you get much done today?

MRS CHAPMAN   I wrote a paper.

MR CHAPMAN   On what?

MRS CHAPMAN   Sex abusers clinics in residential areas.

MR CHAPMAN   Uh huh.

MRS CHAPMAN   They should be God-fearing citizens around
                  here — I was thinking of recommending the
                  Close as a possible future site.

MR CHAPMAN   I see.

MRS CHAPMAN   You wouldn't object, would you Robert?

MR CHAPMAN   I wouldn't, no.

MRS CHAPMAN   Of course not. After all, you've got no kids.

MR CHAPMAN   If this is some kind of blackmail attempt? I
                  can assure you it won't work.

MRS CHAPMAN   Blackmail? Really, Robert. I think you could
                  do with an hour on the couch!

MR CHAPMAN   Well if you are serious about a proposal, my
                  guess is you'll meet with opposition.

MRS CHAPMAN   "Why don't be so horrible Robert, you don't
                  even know them!"

MR CHAPMAN   Like I said, Ellen — it's just a guess.

MRS CHAPMAN   Well a little action around here might
                  brighten things up a bit.

MR CHAPMAN   Another fight, you mean?

MRS CHAPMAN   Well this place sure doesn't need another
                  vegetable.

MR CHAPMAN   I don't imagine anyone accusing you of being
                  a vegetable Ellen — a fruitcase maybe, but a
                  vegetable never!

MRS CHAPMAN   I might contact the council tomorrow. There's
               an empty building on the corner, an old
               Church or something.

MR CHAPMAN   They'll call it heresy.

MRS CHAPMAN   I'm sure they will, they're stupid enough.
               They never want it on their own doorstep but
               are happy enough to move it on to someone
               else's. The fact is these people are already on
               their doorstep only they don't even know it.
               Him next door, he's probably a persistent
               molester but because he's got a "vehicle
               watch" sticker on his car no one would ever
               suspect it. Do they really imagine they're free
               from abuse as long as they don't have a clinic
               on the corner?

MR CHAPMAN   Well you can understand people's feelings on
               the matter.

MRS CHAPMAN   No, you can understand them Robert. I find it
               very difficult.

MR CHAPMAN   So you'd allow your child to play out on the
               streets with an offender's clinic nearby, would
               you?

MRS CHAPMAN   I'm just pointing out the dangers of imagining
               children are safe because nice old Mr Net-
               Twitch is keeping an eye on them.

MR CHAPMAN   You're very unfair.

MRS CHAPMAN   And you are very naive, unless your
               defensiveness is because you have a weakness
               for four year-olds yourself!

MR CHAPMAN   Why do you say such horrible things?

MRS CHAPMAN   Haven't touched a nerve, have I?

MR CHAPMAN   You've touched more than one Ellen — in
               four years of marriage you've managed to
               touch them all and you're getting on all of

them right now! I don't know what I'm
capable of living with you and your case files
— serial killing — child abduction — wife
beating — I've been through them all and it
messes up my head.

MRS CHAPMAN   Oh really? I thought you'd always looked like
that!

Scene Fourteen

That same night. MR *and* MRS PEACH *are sitting on the sofa
playing a board game when there is a sudden loud banging at
the front door.*

MRS PEACH   Harold! Harold!

MR PEACH   Bloody Hell!

MRS PEACH   What do they want Harold?

MR PEACH   They're mad, they're bonkers!

MRS PEACH   But what do they want?

MR PEACH   Get down!

(*He roughly pulls* MRS PEACH *to the ground
and they lay there. The banging stops. They
speak in hushed tones.*)

MRS PEACH   Do you think they've gone?

MR PEACH   I don't know

MRS PEACH   Shall I look?

MR PEACH   No! Stay where you are.

MRS PEACH   We can't stay here all night Harold, I've pork
chops in the oven.

MR PEACH   You and your pork chops. Is that all you care
about, stuffing your porky face with pork
chops is it?!!

(*Slight pause.*)

MRS PEACH	No, Harold.
MR PEACH	Well then shut up and lie still!

(*They continue to lie there for a few moments.*)

MRS PEACH	I can see the skirting needs replacing from here, Harold.
MR PEACH	Oh yes?
MRS PEACH	Yes and there's a chip on the leg of that table Harold, can you see it?
MR PEACH	Where?
MRS PEACH	There look, the back one on your left. Can you see it now, near the foot?
MR PEACH	Ah yes, I see it. A little chip?
MRS PEACH	You can see it if you lie here.
MR PEACH	I've seen it haven't I? I'm seeing it now!
MRS PEACH	Shame isn't it? I was fond of that table.
MR PEACH	I can paint it.
MRS PEACH	It's rosewood, you can't paint rosewood!
MR PEACH	I can.
MRS PEACH	I don't want it painting, I want it replaced!
MR PEACH	Replaced? For a chip on the foot?
MRS PEACH	It might be a chip on the foot now Harold, but if you leave it like that or even paint over it — soon enough and when you're least expecting it that table might collapse and shatter just when you needed it the most.

MR PEACH	What do you mean?
MRS PEACH	I mean do something about it, Harold. Sort it out.
	(MR PEACH *digests the information. They continue to lie there.*)
MR PEACH	I spy with my little eye something beginning with . . . T.
MRS PEACH	Television?
MR PEACH	No.
MRS PEACH	Tape machine?
MR PEACH	No.
MRS PEACH	Table?
MR PEACH	No.
MRS PEACH	Trousers?
MR PEACH	No, you're not even warm.
MRS PEACH	Telephone?
MR PEACH	Yes! Not bad Jean, not bad at all. Here, pass it me.
MRS PEACH	What for?
MR PEACH	Go on, you can reach it from there if you twist . . .
	(*She struggles to reach for the phone and hands it over to* MR PEACH. *He starts dialling a number.*)
MRS PEACH	Who are you ringing?
MR PEACH	It's a surprise.
MRS PEACH	No, don't Harold.

MR PEACH	Why not?
MRS PEACH	Because I don't know what time it is.
MR PEACH	Stop worrying. Leave it to me.

(*He waits a little while.*)

Well where the hell are they then?

MRS PEACH	Like I said — they might be in bed.
MR PEACH	Well they should get out of bed — this is an international call — it could be important for all they know — we'll let it ring for an hour or so while we lie here, shall we?
MRS PEACH	Well if you think it's best, Harold.
MR PEACH	I think it is Jean, yes.

Scene Fifteen

Early in the morning. The Hodges are in their dressing gowns. The phone is ringing and ringing. They are both ignoring it. They look shattered.

MR HODGE	What time is it?
MRS HODGE	Six thirty. Shall I answer it?
MR HODGE	I don't know.
MRS HODGE	Do you want to answer it?
MR HODGE	No, not really.
MRS HODGE	How long will it ring for if we don't answer it?
MR HODGE	Could be a minute, could be an hour.
MRS HODGE	I'll answer it.

(*She picks up the phone.*)

Hello? . . . Hello? . . . Hello there. How are
you? Well the sun's not up yet, but I guess
it'll be hot. Yes, we got it. Yes, thanks. He's
very well. Oh? That's good. Well to be honest
he's still asleep, it's quite early here. Uh huh.
Oh that's nice. Yes he'd like that . . . I said
he'd like that. Ok, if she's there . . . Hello,
how are you? We're fine. Very hot. Is it? Yes
we got it, thanks. Mmmm, it's lovely. Well all
the best. Does he? Ok. Hello again. That
would be great wouldn't it? Yep I'll tell him.
No, no dog, not yet. Yep, we will. You too.
Bye bye.

(*She hangs up.*)

They said they're coming over.

MR HODGE   What?

MRS HODGE   If they win the lottery, they're coming over.

MR HODGE   Shan't hold my breath then.

MRS HODGE   They're trying Jim, they're really trying.

MR HODGE   Did he ask you about a dog?

MRS HODGE   Yes, he wanted to know if we had one yet.

MR HODGE   Cheeky bastard.

MRS HODGE   Go back to bed Jim.

MR HODGE   I can't sleep now, can I?

MRS HODGE   Just give it a go.

MR HODGE   No, we might as well stay up.

                (*She gets up with a sigh.*)

                I bet it's bloody freezing over there.

MRS HODGE   They said it was.

MR HODGE   Shame that, isn't it?

MRS HODGE	Real shame.
MR HODGE	And I bet it's dark and grey and miserable.
MRS HODGE	And boring and lonely and wet, apparently.
MR HODGE	Must be awful.
MRS HODGE	Terrible.
MR HODGE	I can't imagine it.
MRS HODGE	Me neither.
MR HODGE	Shall we do the beach today or the boat?
MRS HODGE	I fancy a sail round the harbour.
MR HODGE	We could send them a photo of us having lunch in the bay.
MRS HODGE	It's the least we can do.
MR HODGE	Under the circumstances.

Scene Sixteen

Latin music fills the stage again. It is the following morning at the Peach's house. MR PEACH *is alone in his living room. He is rehearsing his sales pitch.*

MR PEACH   Morning Madam, or is it Miss? It seems silly not to know considering but I presume it's Madam, nothing to do with your age of course, just because of your husband, it is your husband I take it? Anyway I'm calling in a professional capacity really, I don't know if you realise but I work for one of the country's leading window and door replacement companies and I couldn't help noticing that the windows I sold the previous owners are rather out of date now, I mean it was over eighteen months ago and although they last for life, it struck me that a young couple like yourselves might appreciate something a bit more recent from one of our new lines, like

the Georgian Grand for example, or the
Victoriana? I can leave you a leaflet to show
Mr, eh . . . when he gets home? Or maybe I
could pop round later on this evening to chat
through our obligation-free introductory offer
with him. It doesn't take long, just an hour or
so. How does that sound?

(*Bang!* — *In his head,* MR PEACH *continues
rehearsing.*)

Listen you rich bitch, you either buy some
windows off me now or I'll blow your friggin'
head off! That's right Madam, and you're
friggin' husband's. Get the money — quick! I
want four thousand cash. Now sign this.
Right. It's been a pleasure doing business with
you.

(*He paces around the living room then leaves
through the front door and the lights change
to exterior. He knocks on* MRS CHAPMAN'S
door. She opens it.)

Scene Seventeen

MRS CHAPMAN   Yes?

MR PEACH   (*nervously*) I hope you don't mind me calling
               round, it's just that I couldn't help noticing
               that you'd left a window open and I wanted to
               check that someone was in because there's
               been one or two burglaries in the area in
               recent years and I thought to myself, the last
               thing that young couple need moving into a
               new house is a burglary before they've even
               settled in. I'm Mr Peach from next door, by
               the way. I probably should have said, you must
               have been wondering who I was? Anyway, I
               can see that you are in now so there's no need
               for alarm, probably just wanted some fresh air
               did you? Only I thought that was unlikely
               seeing as it's so COLD.

(He waits to see if she invites him in but she just stands there.)

Anyway, don't want to keep you, you're probably very busy. Right. Ok then. All the best.

(He makes a hasty exit. MRS CHAPMAN slowly closes the front door.)

MRS CHAPMAN   Jesus Christ.

(MR PEACH enters his own house and picks up the telephone and dials.)

MR PEACH   Extension 214, quick as you can. Yes, it's about the notice to cut off my gas. 5434611000F. That's right. It says you're sending someone round today. Well they haven't come. Yes, but you tell me when because I've had to take the morning off work. No, there'll be no one here this afternoon, nor this evening. Well I'll give it another hour and then you can stick it!

(He slams down the phone and paces around for a moment.)

Come on Peach, think!

(He exits through the front door and knocks on MRS CHAPMAN's door. She is working on a paper and has classical music playing. She looks annoyed at the interruption and moves to the window. When she spots MR PEACH she sits down again and resumes working. He bangs on the door again. She ignores it so he manically bangs and bangs on the door until she answers it.)

MRS CHAPMAN   Yes!?

MR PEACH   I'm very sorry to interrupt your morning for a second time and I don't want this to sound

rude, but do you think you could turn your
music down just a little bit, you see I wouldn't
normally ask, well I wouldn't normally be
here, but I've got this terrible headache.

MRS CHAPMAN   Have you tried a hot bath?

MR PEACH   Eh, it's the music you see, it's a bit thumpy
and it's getting on my nerves.

MRS CHAPMAN   You know you want to see a doctor, valium is
still prescribed in acute cases of nervous
disorders.

*(She shuts the door in his face, walks over to
her music system and turns it up. Back in his
house, MR PEACH sits and listens to the
pounding music as the lights fade to black.)*

Scene Eighteen

*When the lights come up MRS PEACH is at home alone. All is
quiet. It is early evening. She is looking through the window
as usual. She swings around and starts pacing the room. She
is cold. She tries to put the fire on but it won't light. She
shivers and pulls her cardigan tightly around herself. She
puts on a record, something hot and Latin and she begins
dancing trying to warm herself up. MR PEACH enters.*

MR PEACH   HERE I AM, JEAN! I'M BACK!

(She jumps with fright.)

MRS PEACH   OH MY GOD! You frightened the life out of me!

MR PEACH   I'm sorry Jean, but I do live here, you know.
Look, I've got a key and everything!

MRS PEACH   There's no need to creep about.

MR PEACH   I was hardly creeping, I was shouting!

MRS PEACH   I didn't hear you.

MR PEACH	No well it's not surprising is it? You were so wrapped up in your dancing. Is that what you get up to while I'm out at work?
MRS PEACH	I was trying to keep warm, the heating doesn't seem to be working.
MR PEACH	You're joking?
	(*He rushes to the fire and starts fiddling with it.*)
MRS PEACH	I've tried it loads of times, I even used a match. Shall we ring the gas board?
MR PEACH	Hang on a minute Jean, let me have a proper look, it might be the pipes or something. I'll have to check upstairs.
MRS PEACH	I thought about asking next door if their gas has been turned off — there might be a leak somewhere in the Close.
MR PEACH	No Jean, gas leaks mean evacuation, you'd have been thrown out.
MRS PEACH	Well what is it then, Harold? I've been freezing!
MR PEACH	I think it might be the ignition knob, I think it might have broken.
MRS PEACH	I couldn't even put the tea on, you'll have to go to the chip shop.
MR PEACH	What do you mean?
MRS PEACH	Well the ignition knob must have broken on the cooker as well — that won't work either!
MR PEACH	Bloody Hell!
MRS PEACH	Harold!

MR PEACH	I'm sorry Jean. I'll have to ring the gas board in the morning — see what the problem is.
MRS PEACH	Won't they send anyone out now?
MR PEACH	It's seven o' clock, there won't be anyone there.
MRS PEACH	Emergency service — 24 hours — the gas board have one, don't they?
MR PEACH	This isn't an emergency though Jean, this is some fault or other. They'll only send them out if there's a leak.
MRS PEACH	Well maybe there was a leak, maybe that's why there's no gas, because it all leaked out.
MR PEACH	Don't be daft Jean, you can smell gas.
MRS PEACH	You'll have to bring that old electric fire down from the loft then.
MR PEACH	Right you are.
MRS PEACH	It would have to happen when the weather's like this. Couldn't happen in the summer, could it? Imagine all those homeless people on the streets with no heating.
MR PEACH	Do I have to?
MRS PEACH	Or old people who can't afford to pay their bills, cause they're on a pension. We're the lucky ones, really. We'll have our heating back on tomorrow. And besides, that old electric fire kicks out some real heat. I'm sure we could live with it for a little while if it's something serious although it doesn't suit the style of the living room, so I wouldn't want to live with it for very long.
MR PEACH	You won't have to. I'll go and get it.
MRS PEACH	Then you'll go for fish and chips?

MR PEACH   Unless you'd rather eat out?

MRS PEACH   No fish and chips will do me fine.

MR PEACH   Right you are.

                  (*He goes upstairs and sits on the bed. He puts his head in his hands.*)

Scene Nineteen

The lights shift to the Chapman's. MR CHAPMAN is home from work. He is pacing the room with a scotch in his hand. MRS CHAPMAN sits on the floor.

MR CHAPMAN   Well if the man had a headache, he had a headache!

MRS CHAPMAN   He's a little Nazi.

MR CHAPMAN   It was a reasonable request, why couldn't you just comply?

MRS CHAPMAN   Because that's you Robert, remember? Robert, born on the Sabbath day, compliant and bonny and good and gay.

MR CHAPMAN   I am not gay.

MRS CHAPMAN   Just impotent.

MR CHAPMAN   Why do you have to be so vindictive? It's not exactly attractive!

MRS CHAPMAN   And what is attractive to you, exactly?

MR CHAPMAN   Please, Ellen . . .

MRS CHAPMAN   I just can't understand why you defend everything.

MR CHAPMAN   Because attacking everything is destructive.

MRS CHAPMAN   But some things need attacking, don't they? Or do you defend Hitler's rise to power?

Mr Chapman	I just don't see the connection between him and the man next door.
Mrs Chapman	That's because you haven't met him yet!
Mr Chapman	He seems harmless enough.
Mrs Chapman	That's what they said about Frederick West.
Mr Chapman	Anyway, don't you think you should be getting ready? The table's booked for eight.
Mrs Chapman	Ok, slave.
Mr Chapman	I am not a slave.
Mrs Chapman	But there must be order in your life, lest you start to enjoy yourself.
Mr Chapman	What is it with you Ellen, why can't you just be nice?
Mrs Chapman	Nice, nice, nice. What is nice? Are you nice?
Mr Chapman	I'm trying to be.
Mrs Chapman	Well try being honest instead. Talk to me.
Mr Chapman	There is no talking to you Ellen, you've got all the answers but you never listen to what I think or I want.
Mrs Chapman	I'm listening now.
Mr Chapman	Well I've nothing to say!
Mrs Chapman	You're frightened of something.
Mr Chapman	You don't know me at all.
Mrs Chapman	Then show me.
Mr Chapman	Why should I?
Mrs Chapman	Because we need to sort things out.

MR CHAPMAN	Sorting things out just means doing everything your way.
MRS CHAPMAN	No it doesn't! You don't come anywhere near me any more!
MR CHAPMAN	Is it surprising?
MRS CHAPMAN	It's confusing.
MR CHAPMAN	Well it shouldn't be with all your snapping and biting.
MRS CHAPMAN	I get angry at you, I can't help it!
MR CHAPMAN	You're always putting me down.
MRS CHAPMAN	Words Robert, just words — I don't even mean half the things I say — I'm just so frustrated!
MR CHAPMAN	Well think before you speak!
MRS CHAPMAN	How am I supposed to do that? I can't censor my thoughts in case you don't like what comes out of my mouth. I can't pussyfoot around you. Sometimes I'm not nice — sometimes I'm very unhappy, that's just the way it comes out. You knew what I was like when you married me.
MR CHAPMAN	You've changed.
MRS CHAPMAN	And so have you.
MR CHAPMAN	How?
MRS CHAPMAN	Why don't you want us to have a baby?
MR CHAPMAN	God, lots of people don't want kids, it's not a crime, you can't keep punishing me.
MRS CHAPMAN	Answer my question!
MR CHAPMAN	Why do you WANT one all of a sudden?

MRS CHAPMAN   I just do!

MR CHAPMAN   Well I just don't!

MRS CHAPMAN   Ever?

MR CHAPMAN   I don't know.

MRS CHAPMAN   Well hazard a guess — might you want one in two years? Five years? Forty five years?

MR CHAPMAN   When I've achieved everything I want to —

MRS CHAPMAN   Oh, well then . . .

MR CHAPMAN   We'll just have to see how it goes.

MRS CHAPMAN   So I'm on trial, am I? If I settle down and buckle under, if I'm sweet and quiet and join in with this nice little place and I stay in the box room studying until I learn how to behave and you get everything in the world you want then maybe, just maybe you'll give me a child — only by that time I'll be barren or dead!

MR CHAPMAN   I haven't got the patience Ellen, I don't want to sit and shake a rattle for hours on end.

MRS CHAPMAN   Then what do you want?

MR CHAPMAN   I want some peace — not a lifetime of responsibility — I can't do it Ellen, I can't bring a child into the world.

MRS CHAPMAN   But I can Robert, I'll look after it, I won't dump it on you if that's what you're scared of.

MR CHAPMAN   No! Ok? No! NO! NO! We always do what you want to do — you want a computer we get a computer — you want a new car we get a new car — you want a baby we get a baby — well not this time!

MRS CHAPMAN   We NEVER do what I want to do! I didn't want to move — you did! I didn't want to come here — you did! I have been compromising since the day we met, that's what people do when they love each other, you don't do anything — you just get drunk!

MR CHAPMAN   Any man would, living with you!

MRS CHAPMAN   Now we're getting somewhere.

MR CHAPMAN   Well what do you expect?! How can I have a child with you when I don't even know if we're going to be together much longer?

(*Short pause.*)

MRS CHAPMAN   Are you planning a separation?

MR CHAPMAN   Look Ellen, you never give anyone a chance, you're harsh, judgemental, it drains me.

MRS CHAPMAN   You like me then?

MR CHAPMAN   I like you — I just don't know if I love you any more.

(*Short pause.*)

MRS CHAPMAN   That makes sense.

MR CHAPMAN   I need a drink.

MRS CHAPMAN   How do you know when your husband is abusing alcohol? As soon as he starts hitting the bottle.

MR CHAPMAN   Ha ha, very funny.

MRS CHAPMAN   I want your baby Robert, it's very important to me.

MR CHAPMAN   I can't help that. It's not my problem.

(*He takes a swig of booze. She sits locked in position.*)

I'll cancel the restaurant, shall I?

Scene Twenty

The lights shift to the Peach's, who are sitting huddled around the electric fire.

MR PEACH	That's better. It's not too bad, now.
MRS PEACH	I think I'll have a steak and kidney pie instead of fish.
MR PEACH	Mushy peas or beans?
MRS PEACH	Mushy peas with a small chips.
MR PEACH	I think I'll have a curry sauce. Warm me up. I'll go in a minute, when I can feel my feet.
MRS PEACH	Wonder what they're having for tea next door . . .
MR PEACH	Probably the same as us. These days the women don't cook so much.
MRS PEACH	I'll bet it's pizza.
MR PEACH	Do you?
MRS PEACH	One of those four cheese ones from Sainsbury's.
MR PEACH	What makes you say that?
MRS PEACH	Just a hunch. We ought to invite them round, I could cook one for them.
MR PEACH	Who, Laurel and Hardy?
MRS PEACH	Don't call them that.
MR PEACH	That's what I'm saying Jean, we've lived next door to them three whole days and we don't even know their names, we can't invite them round for a four cheeses Sainsbury's pizza!

MRS PEACH   Why not? We ought to meet them properly, it
                 makes me feel strange not knowing who we've
                 got on the other side.

MR PEACH   But these things should develop, organically.

MRS PEACH   You didn't say that about Susan and Jim.

MR PEACH   Well Susan and Jim were different.

MRS PEACH   How were they?

MR PEACH   They were friendly, that's all. Those two seem
                 aloof.

MRS PEACH   That's because they're waiting for us.

MR PEACH   Well you can ask them, then.

MRS PEACH   I'll do better than that. I'll invite them,
                 officially.

MR PEACH   You're not going to write to them?

MRS PEACH   I'll make up a little invitation. You can pop it
                 in when you go for the chips.

MR PEACH   If you say so.

MRS PEACH   I do Harold, actually, yes. Six o' clock
                 tomorrow alright with you?

MR PEACH   Well I don't know, do I? I'm on a bit of a roll
                 at the moment.

MRS PEACH   Half past, then.

MR PEACH   I wonder what she does?

MRS PEACH   She's at home all day.

MR PEACH   Is she?

MRS PEACH   You know what I reckon, don't you Harold?

MR PEACH   What?

MRS PEACH	I reckon she might be pregnant.
MR PEACH	Is she a bit . . . bumpy, then, is she?
MRS PEACH	I don't know really, it's more the fact of her being at home and yet I've never heard that hoover go on. Susan and I used to hoover at exactly the same time every afternoon so as not to disturb each other. But I've never heard hers.
MR PEACH	And you deduct from this that she's with child, do you?
MRS PEACH	Well it might account for the music.
MR PEACH	Music?
MRS PEACH	Loud stirring music she had on this afternoon and women go a bit peculiar when they're pregnant. Don't you remember how I got addicted to weepy novels?
MR PEACH	Maybe you're right.
MRS PEACH	Do you think they'll put the nets back up?
MR PEACH	Yes, they'll be giving them a good clean.
MRS PEACH	Only with nets down and lights on you'll be able to see straight in that room.
MR PEACH	That wouldn't be very security conscious, would it? That'd be foolish.
MRS PEACH	You should introduce them to the scheme.
MR PEACH	It's not really my place to.
MRS PEACH	Of course it is. I might introduce her to my catalogue club. I could throw a party, Littlewood's or Kay's.
MR PEACH	I've never understood that about catalogues.
MRS PEACH	What?

MR PEACH   Parties. You don't think they'll be having a
                  house-warming party, do you?

MRS PEACH   Not if she's pregnant.

MR PEACH   And why in the middle of winter do they send
                  you summer catalogues?

MRS PEACH   It's spring/summer, Harold.

MR PEACH   Yes, but I don't understand it — you want to
                  be ordering woolly jumpers in this weather,
                  not bikinis and flip-flops.

MRS PEACH   Well the thing is Harold, you always have to
                  keep one step ahead, otherwise you might get
                  caught out.

                  (*Short pause.*)

MR PEACH   Give us that invite then. I'm going down the
                  chippy.

                  (*He moves to exit as the lights fade to black.*)

                  Scene Twenty One

A spotlight comes up on MR PEACH, *who is centre stage.*

MR PEACH   I was thinking of selling her double-glazing. I
                  even rehearsed the speech but when I got to
                  the door my bottle went. She wore perfume,
                  smelt expensive, not like Jean's. She had these
                  really fascinating lips and I couldn't take my
                  eyes off them, I mean I was doing all the
                  talking but I couldn't stop looking at her lips.
                  Red they were, bright red, not dark red, sultry
                  and stern and sexy I suppose. I babbled on a
                  bit about the open window, she had left it
                  open, inviting it was — I mean anyone could
                  have — if they'd wanted. She didn't speak the
                  first time, just stood there with these lips

pursed together. I shouldn't have done but I
went back a second time, just to hear her
voice, see those lips move and I did have a
headache but her voice kind of soothed it. She
seemed distant somehow, aloof I called it.
This air of class dripped from her, it was quite
stifling, I think I thought I might choke but
once I inhaled it properly, it did, it cleared my
head. I wanted her to ask me in, stand back
from the door and let me through but she
stood her ground. She was giving nothing
away. When she finally shut the door it was a
relief. I think I would have fainted if she
hadn't.

(*Music — "I Don't Want to Play in Your
Yard", by Peggy Lee. Blackout.*)

End of Act One

ACT TWO

Scene One

Music fades out as the lights come up on exterior — Two separate downstage spots. MR PEACH *and* MR CHAPMAN *are arriving home from work at the same time.*

MR CHAPMAN   It's Mr Peach, isn't it?

MR PEACH   That's right, and you are?

MR CHAPMAN   Chapman, Robert Chapman — I think you've met my wife, but we've never been introduced.

MR PEACH   Yes, yes I met her.

MR CHAPMAN   I've been meaning to apologise for not making it to your party the other week. We were both working late.

MR PEACH   It wasn't a party.

MR CHAPMAN   Wasn't it? We got an invitation.

MR PEACH   It was tea for you and your wife — it was Jean's idea, she wanted to welcome you into the Close.

MR CHAPMAN   Oh, I didn't realise — sorry about that.

MR PEACH   Is that your car, is it?

MR CHAPMAN   Yes.

MR PEACH   I notice you haven't got a sticker on it.

MR CHAPMAN   A sticker?

MR PEACH   Vehicle Watch — I run a scheme — you really ought to join, you know.

MR CHAPMAN   Oh, right.

MR PEACH   Come to the next meeting — you can't be too
              careful these days.

MR CHAPMAN   Well it's just my wife — she doesn't agree
              with that sort of thing.

MR PEACH   With what?

MR CHAPMAN   She's a bit of an old hippy at heart, "property
              is theft", and all that.

MR PEACH   I'm not with you.

MR CHAPMAN   By the way, a man called for you the other
              day, he knocked on our door.

MR PEACH   A man?

MR CHAPMAN   Official looking, fair hair — quite a big bloke,
              asking lots of questions.

MR PEACH   Like what?

MR CHAPMAN   Like where you work and what time you'd be
              back.

MR PEACH   And what did you tell him?

MR CHAPMAN   Well nothing, I don't know anything.

MR PEACH   Like I say — there's some very dodgy people
              around, you want to think about
              Neighbourhood Watch — he was probably
              after your place.

MR CHAPMAN   Yes . . . right, well, sorry about the other week.

MR PEACH   No problem.

MR CHAPMAN   See you then.

              (MR CHAPMAN *goes inside.*)

MR PEACH   Not if I see you first.

              (*Snap blackout. Latin music.*)

Scene Two

A few weeks later. It is morning at the Peach's. Much of their furniture is now missing and the old electric fire still remains. MR PEACH *is looking out of the window with a notebook in his hand. The music fades out.*

MRS PEACH	Come away from there Harold — leave them to it. You've got to get ready for work.
MR PEACH	His car's not there again, Jean. (*Writing in his notebook.*) 8:15 AM — no car.
MRS PEACH	They might have gone on holiday.
MR PEACH	Well she hasn't.
MRS PEACH	How do you know?
MR PEACH	I saw her this morning, getting in the milk.
MRS PEACH	He's probably away on business then.
MR PEACH	I warned him about leaving the house with no car outside — people will think they've gone away.
MRS PEACH	Well she's there.
MR PEACH	That's what I'm saying, If anyone broke in she'd be there — on her own.
MRS PEACH	Yes but you're keeping an eye on her for him aren't you?
MR PEACH	Not that he deserves it, refusing to join the scheme.
MRS PEACH	Strange that, wasn't it?
MR PEACH	Stupid you mean. They'd only have to lift the plant pot or look under the mat and bet you they'd find a key. He wouldn't know if he was being watched, surveyed, leaving signs as to

when he's out. Bet he hasn't even got a Chubb
lock or a chain on the door, a hard shove and
a screwdriver and bingo they'd be in, quite
prepared to smash and grab. They could take
anything Jean, TV, stereo, jewellery and she'd
have no defence, and what if they wanted to
teach her a lesson? People can do terrible
things when the impulse takes them. They
could do what they liked with her and leave
her for dead, then just for good measure slash
the curtains and rip the bed clothes and smash
the ornaments and still have time to walk
away with something that wasn't theirs.
That's what happens to people who don't join
the scheme, Jean. I mean what are they then,
some kind of Marxists?

MRS PEACH   I don't suppose she'll want to join the
             catalogue club if she's a Marxist.

MR PEACH   And you wouldn't want her to, Jean! It's
             people like them who make a mockery of hard-
             working folk like us, trying to hang on to
             what's ours. They're just asking for it!

MRS PEACH   Now Harold, don't you go upsetting yourself.

MR PEACH   I'm just saying, Jean — he's been warned.

MRS PEACH   Well I'd better get a move on.

MR PEACH   I'm taking the car in for its MOT this
             morning Jean, did I say?

MRS PEACH   Does David Withers know?

MR PEACH   He's given me the morning to sort it.

MRS PEACH   See you later then. Oh Harold, have you got
             any money? I was going to buy us something
             nice for tea.

MR PEACH   Errr, forgot to go to the cashpoint Jean, I've
             only got my cheque book.

MRS PEACH   It'll have to be soup again then Harold, I don't get paid until Friday.

MR PEACH   I'll try and remember today, Jean.

MRS PEACH   Ok — bye bye.

               (MRS PEACH *exits and* MR PEACH *gets on the telephone*.)

MR PEACH   Yes, I hope so. I'm wanting to sell my car. It's a Montego, six years old. Maroon. Err, it's got about 85,000 on the clock. There's not much wrong with it, a bit of rust on the wheel arch. It's got five months MOT and it's been regularly serviced. Not recent ones, no — well it wasn't done by a garage you see, I serviced it myself — but I am an enthusiast, it's a beautiful little car — never given me a moments trouble, very reliable. Nine hundred or nearest offer. How much? Well why don't I bring it round this morning and you can have a look — I think it's worth a bit more than that mate. Oh I see, fair enough. Can you pay cash? Ok, then — three hundred and fifty cash. I'll be there in half an hour.

               (*He hangs up and exits.* MRS CHAPMAN *is leaving her house at the same time.*)

MR PEACH   Going into town?

MRS CHAPMAN   I might be.

MR PEACH   I can drop you in if you like.

MRS CHAPMAN   No, really.

MR PEACH   It's on my way.

MRS CHAPMAN   No thanks, I'll walk.

MR PEACH   It's no trouble.

MRS CHAPMAN   I said I'll walk.

MR PEACH   Don't you drive yourself, then?

MRS CHAPMAN   No.

MR PEACH   He's away on business, is he?

MRS CHAPMAN   If you say so.

MR PEACH   Don't you go spending all his money, I know
                what you girls are like!

                (*She is gone.* MR PEACH *stares after her.*)

                I know what you're like alright.

                (*He moves inside and gets on the telephone,
                putting his feet up at the table. The
                conversation is clearly one way, he does not
                pause for response.*)

MR PEACH   Jim! It's me, how are you mate? Oh, don't ask
                mate — you've no idea, no idea at all, I mean
                you don't understand mate, well how could
                you? You're there, over there. I mean why
                should you care? You got out just at the right
                time mate — there is no way you'd want your
                wife walking the streets of England — it's not
                safe — it's just not worth it — and you can't
                expect them to walk around like Muslims, this
                is England after all, and in the summer, well,
                the ladies like to feel cool as much as we do
                and why not? . . . the thought of my Jean ever
                being touched by some great brute's big dirty
                hands . . . I mean it, Jim — it keeps me awake
                at night. But they're so naive aren't they?
                They don't even think! But it's happening
                Jim, every day it's happening. This is real life,
                this isn't Australia, mate. This isn't Australia.
                This is real life. This isn't your Bondi Beach
                — oh no, this is here, in this street, this is
                English country garden, we're not accustomed
                — it must have taken some adjusting for you
                has it? All those young things showing what
                they've got? I hope Susan isn't joining in — I
                can't stand it when older women start showing

what they've got, can you? Give her my love
— and Jean's — she misses her you know. A
letter or a phone call wouldn't go amiss. Just
to say hello. Wouldn't hurt. Not like it'd take
up too much time, eh? Eh, Jim? Well . . . I'll
give you a bell. Or drop you another line.
Don't want to lose touch altogether, do we?
Not altogether, looking forward to hearing
from you then, OK? Cheerio.

(*And he hangs up.*)

Scene Three

The lights change to The Hodge's. It is night. Mr Hodge
hangs up the telephone.

Mr Hodge	He's gone crackers.
Mrs Hodge	Well, you know what he's like.
Mr Hodge	That's why I moved to the other side of the world Susan, because I know what he's like.
Mrs Hodge	Just ignore it. Don't answer it any more.
Mr Hodge	And what about all these?

(*He picks up a stack of letters.*)

Mrs Hodge	Well don't open them.
Mr Hodge	I wasn't intending to, but he keeps changing his handwriting, crafty bugger.
Mrs Hodge	Have you had your tablet?
Mr Hodge	I've had three.
Mrs Hodge	Three? That's an overdose Jim, you shouldn't have three!
Mr Hodge	I've been getting palpitations.

MRS HODGE   How about a nice cool drink to calm you down.

MR HODGE   Is the air conditioning on?

MRS HODGE   It's up as far as it'll go — why don't you have a lie down?

MR HODGE   Why should I have a lie down? I haven't come over here to lie down, I've come to enjoy myself — live a little.

MRS HODGE   You can't let them get to you like this, Jim — they're far, far away.

MR HODGE   But they'll get here, Susan — I can feel it — they'll get here, eventually.

MRS HODGE   Don't be so daft. You know Jean spends all his money.

MR HODGE   What if he's got a nest egg he hasn't told her about?

MRS HODGE   What? She'd have sniffed that out by now — she's no fool, take my word for it.

MR HODGE   Ice cream, I could eat an ice cream.

MRS HODGE   I'll make you a Sundae with a cherry on the top.

(Aborigine music rises in the blackout and fades out as the lights come up on the next scene.)

Scene Four

Early evening exterior — two downstage spotlights. MRS PEACH *is returning home from work as* MRS CHAPMAN *is returning home from town.* MRS CHAPMAN *carries several Mothercare bags. She is trying to find her keys.*

MRS PEACH   Can I give you a hand?

MRS CHAPMAN   I'm perfectly capable of letting myself into my own house.

MRS PEACH   I could hold the bags for you.

              (MRS CHAPMAN *ignores her.*)

              They're really expensive these days aren't they? In my day we had all hand-me-downs.

              (MRS CHAPMAN *still struggles to find them.*)

              It's when they hit six or seven that the real cost starts, then they want all sorts off the telly.

              (MRS CHAPMAN *finds her keys and turns to look at* MRS PEACH.)

MRS CHAPMAN   Will you shut up!

              (*And she disappears out of her spotlight and into the house, slamming the front door behind her. The lights cross-fade into the inside of the Peach's.* MRS PEACH *appears upset. She sits down trembling a little. Suddenly music starts up from next door. A loud, thumping classical rhythm. She looks concerned but tries to ignore it. She takes off her coat and shoes and puts on her slippers. She settles down on the sofa and closes her eyes. She puts her hands over her ears as lights fade down to black. The music thumps on in the blackout before fading out.*)

                        Scene Five

MRS PEACH *is asleep on the sofa when the lights come up. All is quiet.* MR PEACH *enters.*

MR PEACH   HELLO-*O!*

              (MRS PEACH *wakes up with a start.*)

MRS PEACH   Harold?

MR PEACH   You want to see what they've done to his car
               out here.

MRS PEACH   Oh, he's back then?

MR PEACH   They've only scratched his bonnet!

MRS PEACH   Who has?

MR PEACH   Must have been kids — I knew something like
               this would happen.

MRS PEACH   Oh dear!

MR PEACH   Can you believe it, Jeannie?

MRS PEACH   Is it very bad?

MR PEACH   Un-repeatable!

MRS PEACH   What do you mean?

MR PEACH   They've scratched something very offensive.

MRS PEACH   They haven't!

MR PEACH   Well he can't say I didn't warn him.

               (MR PEACH *takes off his coat and holds out a
               Sainsbury's carrier bag.*)

               I've got a surprise for you in here.

MRS PEACH   What is it?

MR PEACH   A four cheese Sainsbury's pizza!

MRS PEACH   What for?

MR PEACH   For tea! I went and bought it specially.

MRS PEACH   But I don't like pizza.

MR PEACH   Oh, I thought you did . . . oh well, never
                mind. I'll take you out for dinner if you like?

                (MRS PEACH *starts crying.*)

                Eh! — eh! — what's all this for?

MRS PEACH   I don't feel very well.

MR PEACH   What's wrong?

MRS PEACH   I burnt the Toad-in-the-Hole at school so the
                kids wouldn't eat it and the bus was late and
                the woman next door was really rude to me
                and then I had to listen to her music and now
                I've got a headache and I want my table back!

MR PEACH   Oh dear, oh dear, oh dear — you have got
                yourself into a state haven't you?

MRS PEACH   I really miss it, Harold.

MR PEACH   I did tell you the waiting list was long.

MRS PEACH   Can't you take it somewhere else?

MR PEACH   It's in line now, it would be silly to start again
                somewhere else.

MRS PEACH   But it was only a chip on the foot.

MR PEACH   I'll get you a sherry.

MRS PEACH   We've run out.

MR PEACH   Damn, I meant to replace that bottle — I'll do
                it tomorrow.

MRS PEACH   I was only trying to be friendly you know, I
                wasn't being nosey.

MR PEACH   About what?

MRS PEACH   About the baby . . . she looked like she was
                going to kill me and she told me to shut up!

MR PEACH   Maybe it's her hormones playing up, you said
                yourself they go peculiar. Don't take any
                notice of her — they've got their comeuppance
                with that lot outside.

MRS PEACH   Did you take our car to the garage?

MR PEACH   I did.

MRS PEACH   When can we have it back?

MR PEACH   Oh, give it a couple of weeks. Here you are . . .
                you have that and buy yourself something nice
                tomorrow.

                (*He gives her some cash out of his wallet.*)

MRS PEACH   Are you sure, Harold?

MR PEACH   Course I am. Now, I'd better get rid of this
                pizza.

MRS PEACH   No don't waste it. I'll pop it round there and
                see if they want it.

MR PEACH   After the way she treated you?

MRS PEACH   Well I was probably being unfair — I forgot
                about the hormones, it might make her feel
                better — cheer her up.

MR PEACH   I don't know — they don't deserve us, do
                they?

                (*Blackout.*)

Scene Six

Inside the Chapman's.

MR CHAPMAN   ELLEN! ELLEN! ELLEN!

                (MRS CHAPMAN *appears in her dressing gown.*)

MR CHAPMAN   You might have come down when I called. It
               was you she wanted to see! She brought you a
               pizza.

MRS CHAPMAN   How yummy.

MR CHAPMAN   I didn't know you'd spoken to her.

MRS CHAPMAN   You didn't ask.

MR CHAPMAN   She thinks you're ill, what did you say to her?

MRS CHAPMAN   Nothing.

MR CHAPMAN   Are you staying in the box room?

MRS CHAPMAN   Is there any point in me moving back in?

MR CHAPMAN   Not really, no.

MRS CHAPMAN   Then I'll stay in the box room.

MR CHAPMAN   She thinks I should report the car to the
               police.

MRS CHAPMAN   Why don't you?

MR CHAPMAN   You tell me.

MRS CHAPMAN   What's that supposed to mean?

MR CHAPMAN   I just don't think that's a very good idea do
               you?

MRS CHAPMAN   So live with it, it's not the end of the world.

MR CHAPMAN   I'll have to get it repaired. I'm not going into
               work with "Fuck Face" inscribed on my
               bonnet.

MRS CHAPMAN   Why not? I think it suits you.

               (*Blackout. Latin music.*)

Scene Seven

Music fades out. It is the next morning at the Peach's. MR
PEACH *is looking out of the window again with his notebook.*

MR PEACH	Look at him. He won't get rid of it like that.
MRS PEACH	I still think she could have said thank you.
MR PEACH	Ungrateful, ignorant, that's all they are. Ha! Ha! He's making it worse now! . . . That's it . . . give up, mate. It'll need a professional that will, I'm telling you. He should have had a sticker . . . I told you to get a sticker! Idiot!
MRS PEACH	Come away Harold — he'll see you.
MR PEACH	8:40 AM — Chapman cannot leave for work due to obscene vandalism on car.
MRS PEACH	Maybe I got it wrong, maybe they don't like pizza.
MR PEACH	Any post this morning?
MRS PEACH	Plenty for you, nothing for me.
MR PEACH	Where is it then?
MRS PEACH	Over there, all bills by the looks of it.
MR PEACH	Oh yes?
MRS PEACH	That blouse I ordered didn't come.
MR PEACH	I'll ring them tomorrow.
MRS PEACH	They promised it would come today, I was looking forward to it.
MR PEACH	Well I've given you some money haven't I? That's what it's for, so you can buy yourself something.
MRS PEACH	I liked the one in the catalogue.

MR PEACH   Well give me the money back then, there's no
              point in having it if you aren't going to spend it!

              (*Short pause.*)

MRS PEACH   How are things going at work, Harold?

MR PEACH   Fine.

MRS PEACH   You're doing alright?

MR PEACH   Better than most.

MRS PEACH   Only some of those bills are marked "final
              notice".

MR PEACH   Been studying them, have you?

MRS PEACH   No.

MR PEACH   It's not every middle-aged man can walk out
              of redundancy and into a job.

MRS PEACH   I know that.

MR PEACH   You want to count yourself lucky. There's
              many a proud man being forced on the dole,
              robbing Peter to pay Paul. It's not like it was.
              I've seen poverty make whores of women and
              robbers of men — you've got a roof over your
              head and you want to be grateful.

MRS PEACH   I am grateful Harold . . . I'm just concerned.

MR PEACH   There is nothing for you to be concerned
              about. I've got us this far, haven't I?

MRS PEACH   I know you have Harold, I know you have. Can
              I get anything for you? Is there anything you'd
              like?

MR PEACH   You spend it on yourself — that's what it's for.

MRS PEACH   Are you coming with me to get the bus?

MR PEACH   I thought I might make a start down this
              street. It's been a while since I've tried it.

MRS PEACH   Do you know what time you'll be back?

MR PEACH   That all depends on how I do.

MRS PEACH   I'll see you later then.

              (MRS PEACH *is about to leave.*)

MR PEACH   Oh Jean . . .

MRS PEACH   Yes Harold.

MR PEACH   You do know how much I love you?

MRS PEACH   Yes, I think so.

MR PEACH   Good. That's very important to me.

MRS PEACH   Cheerio.

              (*She exits and he goes and picks up the morning's bills.*)

MR PEACH   SHIT!

              (*The lights fade down on him and classical music fills the air.*)

Scene Eight

Music fades out as lights come up. Same morning at the Chapman's. MRS CHAPMAN is sitting in the living room in her dressing gown. She is curled up on the sofa with a couple of soft toys. She is awake but lying still, staring into space. MR CHAPMAN enters from outside.

MR CHAPMAN   It's no good, I've tried everything, it's not going to come off.

              (*He studies her for awhile.*)

              Are you going to do some work today?

              (*She shrugs her shoulders.*)

Only I don't think regressing to a two year old
is very good for you, do you?

(*She shakes her head miserably.*)

Well are you going to get dressed?

(*She sits up slowly but once upright she just
stares at the floor, motionless.*)

You can't carry on like this, Ellen. It's not
fair on me. I really think you ought to see
somebody, one of your colleagues might be
able to help you. Will you promise me you'll
think about it?

(*She nods her head.*)

At least try and occupy your mind with
something else. Do some gardening, it's a
lovely day. I've got to go now. I'll see you
tonight.

(*He goes to leave, turns and looks back at her
once more before leaving the house and
meeting up with* MR PEACH *outside the front.*
MR CHAPMAN *is itching to get to work but* MR
PEACH *holds him up. The scene takes place in
the spotlights, downstage.*)

MR PEACH	Morning!
MR CHAPMAN	Morning.
MR PEACH	Just having a look at the state of your car.
MR CHAPMAN	It won't come off.
MR PEACH	Well have you tried that tinted polish? It might work if you put it on thick.
MR CHAPMAN	No, I think I'll take it in to a garage.
MR PEACH	(*drawing a breath*) It'll cost you, that will.
MR CHAPMAN	Well — not to worry.

MR PEACH   I don't know — kids, eh? Mind you this sort
                of thing doesn't usually happen around here.
                They know we keep an eye out you see, but
                with you not having a sticker, well I suppose
                they thought they could get away with it.

MR CHAPMAN   Yes, probably it was the sticker, yes in fact
                I'm sure it was the sticker, the sticker would
                have saved it, the sticker would have protected
                it, if only I'd had a sticker!!!

MR PEACH   Nice day, isn't it?

MR CHAPMAN   Look, I've really got to go . . .

                (*He starts to move off.*)

MR PEACH   Hang on! I've been meaning to pop one of
                these round to you.

                (*He waves a printed document at* MR
                CHAPMAN.)

MR CHAPMAN   Oh . . . right.

                (MR CHAPMAN *takes it and glances at it.*)

MR PEACH   It's a very exciting new deal my firm is
                offering, I think you'll find it attractive and
                you'll also find some information in there
                about window and door security as well,
                different locks and shutters, etc. I mean now
                you've had this nasty experience you might
                like to think about it, that's all.

MR CHAPMAN   Er, thanks very much but I think we're alright
                as we are . . . I've got to go . . .

                (*He hands it back to* MR PEACH.)

MR PEACH   Take it with you — no rush, look over it in
                your own time.

MR CHAPMAN   No honestly, there wouldn't be any point, we're not interested in windows or locks or stickers OK?! Sorry about that!

(And he is gone. MR PEACH screws up the document.)

MR PEACH   *(to himself)* Oh, that's alright mate, don't you worry about it, you just look after Number One.

(He shakes his head and leaves the spotlight as it fades to black.)

Scene Nine

Aborigine music as lights come up on the Hodge's. It is night.

MR HODGE   *(reading)* And the seeds are going to produce another fantastic crap this summer.

MRS HODGE   It's crop, another fantastic crop this summer.

MR HODGE   He hasn't written crop though has he?

MRS HODGE   Let me have a look . . . no, he's written crap.

MR HODGE   He must be losing his eyesight as well as his marbles. I wonder if he'll send us any of his crap pansies this year.

MRS HODGE   I wouldn't be surprised.

MR HODGE   Doesn't he realise they die in the post?

MRS HODGE   Obviously not.

MR HODGE   And what the hell is an all-in-one hat and scarf?

MRS HODGE   I've no idea.

MR HODGE   Poor Jean, I feel sorry for her really. It's not her fault she's married to him.

MRS HODGE   Well whose fault is it then?

MR HODGE   You know what I mean, I don't think she's the full shift.

MRS HODGE   Make an ideal couple then don't they?

MR HODGE   Yes, but she wasn't always so odd was she? He got to her, that's what I mean.

MRS HODGE   Oh well then, if you're so concerned for her welfare, invite her over, pay for her flight.

MR HODGE   You must be joking!

MRS HODGE   I am actually Jim, yes.

MR HODGE   I should hope so.

MRS HODGE   Mind you, it'd be almost worth it just to see the look on Harold's face.

MR HODGE   It'd kill him wouldn't it?

MRS HODGE   That settles it then — I'll book her on the next flight out!

                 (*And they both manage a smile as the lights fade out.*)

Scene Ten

Classical music is playing softly. When the lights come back up it is evening at the Chapman's. MR CHAPMAN *is reading a newspaper.* MRS CHAPMAN *enters the room wearing a bikini under her robe. She stands behind him. He looks up from his newspaper.*

MR CHAPMAN   Oh, you're in.

                 (*He goes back to reading.*)

                 I called you, didn't you hear me?

MRS CHAPMAN   I was up in my room.

MR CHAPMAN   Oh, I see. You haven't done any work again
               today then?

MRS CHAPMAN   I did go out in the garden this morning.

MR CHAPMAN   (*distracted*) Oh good, very good.

MRS CHAPMAN   I just lay down on the grass to have a sunbathe
               and a think.

MR CHAPMAN   That's something anyway.

MRS CHAPMAN   And then it started getting hot so I took my
               top off for a bit, I mean I didn't think anyone
               could see me, so I closed my eyes for a second
               and when I opened them again he was there in
               his garden pretending to weed some plants but
               I knew what he was looking at Robert, I could
               tell by the way his hands were shaking.

               (MR CHAPMAN *slowly puts down his
               newspaper.*)

               I put my top back on and came inside and
               watched him for a bit through the open
               window. I caught his eye and he disappeared
               back in his house. After that every time I
               stepped out in the garden he'd appear
               suddenly and it couldn't have been
               coincidence, there were just too many
               occasions so I gave up eventually and went
               upstairs. I lay on the bed and fantasised about
               him being put away somewhere with high
               security walls that he couldn't see over and he
               was waiting for Mrs Net-Twitch to visit him,
               but of course, she never did.

               (*Pause.*)

MR CHAPMAN   To be perfectly honest, Ellen I'm beginning to
               think it's you that needs the high security unit
               — after all, it is his garden, he does have a
               right to weed his plants!!

(*And he pulls a soft toy from the sofa, stands up and flings it across the room. Then he marches off, pushing past* MRS CHAPMAN *who remains where she is as the lights and music fade out.*)

Scene Eleven

Same evening at the Peach's. MRS PEACH *is dusting her table which has miraculously appeared again, but the chip on the foot still remains. She is cheerful and the evening sunlight atmospherically lights the stage.*

MRS PEACH   I've found you the shears if you want to clip the hedge.

MR PEACH   Where were they then?

MRS PEACH   At the back of the shed. They're alright I think, not too blunt.

MR PEACH   Right you are.

MRS PEACH   It's a lovely evening for it anyway. I dread to think what Jim would say if he could see the state of their garden.

MR PEACH   He knows all about it.

MRS PEACH   You've spoken to him, then?

MR PEACH   I wrote him a letter, I sent your love.

MRS PEACH   We ought to get them some weed killer.

MR PEACH   Look where that got us last time.

MRS PEACH   It wasn't your fault the dog drank it, how were you to know it was his drinking bucket? Anyway, that constant yap-yap-yap-yapping got on my nerves and it was a vicious little thing, remember that time it bit you?

MR PEACH   Of course I do — it drew blood!

MRS PEACH	You should go and have a look at all the rubbish they've got out there. Rows and rows of bin bags. God only knows how two people can create so much waste.
MR PEACH	He wants to get them cleared before I get on to the council — what if they came open? — we could have all sorts of junk flying about the place and anyway they're an eyesore, it's a bloody disgrace!
MRS PEACH	Your pansies are coming up nicely this year though. Beautiful they are. I think they're your best yet.
MR PEACH	Do you?
MRS PEACH	Oh definitely. I'm going to take a photograph of them and send it to the Hodges.
MR PEACH	It'll only make them home-sick, Jean.
MRS PEACH	Well, it's not everyone who can grow pansies like you, Harold — you're the best.
MR PEACH	No thanks to that lot . . .
MRS PEACH	Maybe this time the Hodges will write back.
MR PEACH	Well they're probably very busy, Jean — lots to do in Australia.
MRS PEACH	I'd love to see their house.
MR PEACH	Maybe you will do one day.
MRS PEACH	Oh well, best get on.
MR PEACH	Right you are.

(*She plugs in the hoover and starts hoovering around as he just sits there staring into space. Lights fade down.*)

Scene Twelve

Same evening inside the Chapman's. Mr CHAPMAN *enters carrying a stack of baby clothes and teddies in his arms.* MRS CHAPMAN *still in her dressing gown looks depressed.*

MR CHAPMAN   Right, you are going to tell me right now why you have been buying all this stuff!

MRS CHAPMAN   I can't help it.

MR CHAPMAN   Of course you can! Look at them Ellen, LOOK AT THEM! You can't can you? Because you know how sick it is! Why do you do it?

MRS CHAPMAN   I don't know.

MR CHAPMAN   So suddenly Mrs Know-it-all knows nothing!

(*Short pause.*)

MRS CHAPMAN   Why don't you believe me about Mr Peach? In fact why are you still here?

MR CHAPMAN   What?

MRS CHAPMAN   Why haven't you moved out?

MR CHAPMAN   Is that why you do it, to try and drive me out?!

MRS CHAPMAN   You tell me you don't love me any more, you tell me I'm nuts, you sneak into my room and steal my things and yet you make no moves to leave me — I just want to know what's keeping you here.

MR CHAPMAN   It's our home.

MRS CHAPMAN   No it isn't. It's just a house — you could sell it — buy another.

MR CHAPMAN   I don't know if I'm ready for that.

MRS CHAPMAN   Do you want me to leave?

MR CHAPMAN   No, I want you to stop all — this!

Mrs Chapman	And if I could — what then?
Mr Chapman	Maybe we could sort something out.
Mrs Chapman	Like divorce?
Mr Chapman	If you can just accept me as I am and live without a baby then maybe we can make it work.
Mrs Chapman	And if I can't?
Mr Chapman	I don't know.
Mrs Chapman	Would it be so terrible to have my child?
Mr Chapman	You're going to have to pull yourself together.
Mrs Chapman	Come with me to counselling.
Mr Chapman	You're a fucking therapist — you sort it out! I'm getting rid of these.
Mrs Chapman	No Robert!

(*She struggles to get the things off him.*)

Mr Chapman	Just grow up will you, or go and get yourself some help!
Mrs Chapman	They're mine!
Mr Chapman	RIGHT!

(*He gets a bin bag and begins piling the stuff inside while she stands and watches, clutching a teddy bear she managed to retrieve. He drags the bag off as she holds the teddy to her chest and the tears roll down her face.*)

Scene Thirteen

Inside the Peach's. Mrs Peach is just putting the vacuum away. Mr Peach is at the window overlooking the garden.

MR PEACH	Jean! Jean! Come and look at this! Can you believe it? Pass me the camera — I'm getting this on film . . . LOOK AT HIM! HE'S SETTING FIRE TO THE BIN BAGS!
MRS PEACH	MY WASHING!
MR PEACH	GET THE CAMERA — QUICK!!!
	(MRS PEACH *fumbles for the camera and passes it to* MR PEACH, *who starts snapping away*.)
MRS PEACH	Shall I get the washing in?
MR PEACH	No leave it there Jean — it's evidence!
MRS PEACH	But Harold, the smoke will ruin it!
MR PEACH	BLOODY HELL! LOOK AT THE SIZE OF THESE FLAMES!
MRS PEACH	Why doesn't he just take them down the tip like everyone else?
MR PEACH	Because he obviously thinks he can do what he likes . . . JESUS CHRIST!
MRS PEACH	What's happening?
MR PEACH	OI! CHAPMAN! GET OFF THERE!
MRS PEACH	What's he doing?
MR PEACH	HE'S STEPPING ON MY PANSIES — HE'S GOT HIS GREAT CLODHOPPERS OVER A WHOLE PATCH OF THEM!
MRS PEACH	He's not doing it on purpose, he's trying to put the flames out.
MR PEACH	I don't care, I'm not having that!
MRS PEACH	Don't, Harold!
MR PEACH	Get out of my way Jean!
	(*He exits*.)

MRS PEACH   No Harold!

                   (*The lights quickly change to the exterior
                   spots.* MR PEACH *has rushed outside and smoke
                   is drifting across the stage.* MR CHAPMAN *is
                   out of breath.*)

MR PEACH   What the hell do you think you're doing?

MR CHAPMAN   Sorry, the flames were getting out of hand.

MR PEACH   Get your feet off my flowers!

MR CHAPMAN   They're not on your flowers.

MR PEACH   That's one of my pansies under your foot!

MR CHAPMAN   There are your pansies — I'm nowhere near
                   them.

MR PEACH   Move your feet.

MR CHAPMAN   Alright!

MR PEACH   Cheeky bastard!

MR CHAPMAN   Look, just mind your own business, will you?

MR PEACH   It is my business if you're wrecking our
                   washing and stepping on my flowers — I'm
                   reporting you to the council — I've got it all
                   on film!

MR CHAPMAN   I can do without this to be honest.

MR PEACH   Yeah I bet you can, treating your garden like a
                   rubbish tip — it's a bloody disgrace!

MR CHAPMAN   And what would you know about it?

MR PEACH   You live like pigs, the pair of you!

MR CHAPMAN   How dare you!

MR PEACH   And she plays her music all day upsetting my
                   wife — it's disgusting — she might be
                   pregnant but there's no need for it!

MR CHAPMAN	My wife is NOT pregnant so mind your own business!
MR PEACH	Of course she's pregnant, you stupid idiot!
MR CHAPMAN	I don't know what you're talking about but if you don't shut up I'll belt you one!

(*He shoves* MR PEACH.)

MR PEACH	Get your hands off me — I'll have you for assault!
MR CHAPMAN	That wasn't assault — THIS IS!

(MR CHAPMAN *punches* MR PEACH. *So* MR PEACH *hits him back. The two men tussle together for a while.* MRS PEACH *can be heard shouting.*)

MRS PEACH	HAROLD! FOR GOD'S SAKE! LEAVE HIM ALONE!
MR PEACH	LOOK AT MY PANSIES — THEY'RE RUINED NOW — HE'S KILLED THEM! HE'S KILLED MY PANSIES, YOU — MURDERER!

(*And he takes another dive at* MR CHAPMAN. *So* MR CHAPMAN *grabs a handful of pansies and stuffs them down* MR PEACH'S *front.* MRS PEACH *enters and drags her husband off. He is sobbing.*)

MRS PEACH	(*to* MR CHAPMAN) You ought to be ashamed of yourself!

(MR CHAPMAN *takes another dive at* MR PEACH *and this time* MRS PEACH *gets tangled up in the struggle. There is much shouting and chaos drowned out by loud "Gypsy Kings" music and the lights fade down on the scene. The music continues in the blackout then fades as the lights come up on the next scene.*)

Scene Fourteen

Back inside the Chapman's. MR CHAPMAN *has a drink in his hand and* MRS CHAPMAN *is trying to control her laughter.*

MR CHAPMAN   It's not funny!

MRS CHAPMAN   I'm sorry.

MR CHAPMAN   Well you should be — it's your fault!

MRS CHAPMAN   Did he hurt you?

MR CHAPMAN   He kicked me!

                (*She laughs again.*)

MRS CHAPMAN   Oh, I'm sorry Robert.

MR CHAPMAN   He's a bloody nutter!

MRS CHAPMAN   I told you he was.

MR CHAPMAN   I was nowhere near his bloody pansies.

MRS CHAPMAN   There was no need to punch him.

MR CHAPMAN   Who does he think he is? STUPID ARSE!

MRS CHAPMAN   He's probably phoning the police.

MR CHAPMAN   Let him! He started it. He came out really aggressive — there was no need for it and they obviously think you're pregnant.

MRS CHAPMAN   What do you mean?

MR CHAPMAN   I should have KILLED HIM while I had the chance!

MRS CHAPMAN   Alright — calm down!

MR CHAPMAN   Why should I? It's my garden I'll do what the hell I like in it!

MRS CHAPMAN   Like burn my things.

MR CHAPMAN   Well what do you expect me to do?! Just sit
              back and let you shop for a baby that doesn't
              exist! Take no notice of the fact that you've
              turned the study into a nursery — that you've
              prams and cots and mobiles all over the house!
              And how much is it all costing?

MRS CHAPMAN   Oh I might have known money would come
              into it — it's my money.

MR CHAPMAN   And the fact I work my balls off all day counts
              for nothing I suppose — we're supposed to be
              putting it into the house!

MRS CHAPMAN   You put your earnings into the house and I'll
              spend my money on what the hell I like!

MR CHAPMAN   But it's not normal, Ellen.

MRS CHAPMAN   And it's not normal that a husband can just
              ignore his wife's feelings!

              (*The telephone rings.*)

              It's probably them.

MR CHAPMAN   Well I'm not answering it.

MRS CHAPMAN   It might be your "ex".

MR CHAPMAN   Well you answer it then!

MRS CHAPMAN   Why should I? It's your "ex"!

              (MR CHAPMAN *picks the phone up.*)

MR CHAPMAN   Yes?

              (*He hangs up.*)

              Here we go — they've started with the funny
              phone calls now. (*To the wall.*) Psycho!

              (MR CHAPMAN *gets another drink.*)

MRS CHAPMAN   Don't have another one, Robert.

MR CHAPMAN   Why not?

MRS CHAPMAN   Because it doesn't do any good.

MR CHAPMAN   It does ME good, I can tell you! I've been
              nothing but civil to them since the day we
              moved in — it's YOU that's upset them!

MRS CHAPMAN   I haven't ruined their flowers and beaten them
              up!

MR CHAPMAN   No but you've been playing your music loudly,
              upsetting his wife — he told me!

MRS CHAPMAN   It's not my fault you brought me to a house
              with paper-thin walls — I LIKE MY MUSIC
              LOUD!!!

MR CHAPMAN   WELL IF THEY THOUGHT THAT WAS
              LOUD THEY WANT TO LISTEN TO THIS!

              (MR CHAPMAN *puts on music that is
              deafeningly loud, then pours himself another
              drink.* MRS CHAPMAN *knocks the drink out of
              his hand and they struggle for a moment. He
              clasps her wrists tightly.*)

MRS CHAPMAN   Robert, you're hurting me!

              (*He pulls her towards him and kisses her, she
              resists so he pulls the back of her head
              towards him and kisses her again. He lets go
              of her wrists and the two kiss each other
              passionately and hold each other as the lights
              fade down to black.*)

                          Scene Fifteen

Inside the Peach's. The music is thumping. MR PEACH *sits in
silence, very still.* MRS PEACH *paces around.*

MRS PEACH   Shut up shut up shut up shut up shut up shut
              up shut up shut up shut up shut up shut up

shut up shut up shut up shut up shut up shut
up shut up shut up shut up shut up shut up
SHUT UP SHUT UP SHUT UP SHUT — UP!!

(*The music continues.*)

Help help help help help help help help help
help help help help help help help help help
help help help help help help help help help
help help help help help help help HELP
HELP HELP! HELP! HELP! *H E L P!*

(*She begins dancing to the music delicately,
trying to use it so that it doesn't affect her.
After some time she stops and mutters.*)

She acts and I react — act and react, act and
react, act back, ACT BACK, ACT BACK!

(*She smashes an ornament against the wall.
The music stops.* MR PEACH *looks over.*)

MR PEACH   What's going on? What have you done? What
                time is it?

MRS PEACH   Four o' clock — I thought it was going to go
                on all night!

MR PEACH   Shall we go to bed now?

MRS PEACH   It hardly seems worth it — I have to be up in a
                couple of hours.

MR PEACH   How can they stand it? That's what I'd like to
                know.

MRS PEACH   They've probably taken sleeping pills so they
                can sleep through it.

MR PEACH   Let's hope they've taken hundreds so they
                never wake up again!

MRS PEACH   Do you want another pain killer?

                (*He shakes his head.*)

I still can't believe he punched you. He wants
locking up. Why won't you call the police?

MR PEACH   I'll sort him out my own way.

MRS PEACH   I think we should consider moving.

MR PEACH   You what?

MRS PEACH   I think we should look around for another
house.

MR PEACH   You must be joking!

MRS PEACH   Things have never been the same since Jim
and Susan left and now with all this I think
we should go.

MR PEACH   They'll get me out of here over my dead body.

MRS PEACH   I'm frightened, Harold.

MR PEACH   I'll sort it out, Jean — my own way.

                (*He moves to the telephone and starts dialling
                a number.*)

MRS PEACH   What are you doing?

MR PEACH   Ssssh! . . . Oh, bloody typical — they won't
answer!

                (*He slams down the receiver.*)

MRS PEACH   Well they know you'll give them "what for",
don't they? — that's why they're not
answering.

MR PEACH   Right!

MRS PEACH   Now who are you ringing?

MR PEACH   No! No! No!

                (*He slams down the receiver again.*)

They've left it off the hook haven't they?
That's what they've done — devious little
bastards!

MRS PEACH   Harold, stop it — STOP IT!

(MR PEACH *dials again.*)

MR PEACH   Yes. I want you to intercept a call — it is an
emergency — it's constantly engaged and I
need to get through. It IS a matter of life and
death! I DEMAND YOU INTERCEPT IT!
YOU'RE THE OPERATOR, OF COURSE
YOU CAN! I'LL TELL YOU EXACTLY
WHY IT'S A MATTER OF LIFE AND
DEATH, BECAUSE IF YOU DON'T
INTERCEPT THIS CALL I'M GONNA BLOW
YOUR FRIGGIN' HEAD OFF YOUR
SHOULDERS!!!

(*He turns to* JEAN.)

I don't believe it! She hung up! A public
service and she hung up! RIGHT, I'm ringing
the Hodges.

MRS PEACH   What for?

MR PEACH   They sold them the bloody house — selfish
pigs — pissing off to Australia and leaving us
with LUNATICS!

MRS PEACH   I'm not having this — I'm going to see an
estate agent in the morning — I'm not having
this! NOW PUT THE PHONE DOWN!

MR PEACH   Hello, I'd like to report a house fire please. 37
Appleacre Crescent. No I'd rather not.

(*He hangs up.*)

MRS PEACH   What did you do that for?

(*He dials again.*)

MRS PEACH   Tell them you made a mistake — I mean it,
Harold.

MR PEACH   Police please. I'd like to report a prowler. 37
                Appleacre Crescent — please hurry.

                (*He hangs up.*)

MRS PEACH   NOW STOP IT! THAT'S ENOUGH!

MR PEACH   Yes I'd like to order a taxi please for 37
                Appleacre Crescent — going to the Bishop's
                Psychiatric Hospital. Chapman. Thank you.

MRS PEACH   You're only upsetting yourself.

                (MR PEACH *stands up and kicks the telephone
                before collapsing into a heap on the floor.*
                MRS PEACH *joins him and puts her arms
                around him as lights fade to black.*)

                        Scene Sixteen

The Hodges are at home when the telephone rings.

MR HODGE   Oh bloody hell!

MRS HODGE   Just ignore it Jim, don't answer it.

MR HODGE   It won't stop — ever.

                (MRS HODGE *snatches up the telephone.*)

MRS HODGE   Yes? Look Jean, it's very expensive to keep
                phoning here. What do you want? I'm sorry?
                Well he can't Jean, I mean there aren't any
                grounds. Now don't get into a state just take
                my word for it, nothing's going to happen . . .
                Ok? Ok. They go a bit funny at that age, you
                just let him get on with it. Well what do you
                think of them? Well why don't you try talking
                to her? Well then — move. Well then leave
                him there and you move. Look Jean, I don't
                know what to say to you, there really isn't
                anything I can do from over here. You'll have
                to brave it. I'm sorry Jean. Bye.

(*She hangs up.*)

She say's Harold is going to sue us.

MR HODGE	What?
MRS HODGE	For selling our house to lunatics.
MR HODGE	What's he talking about now?
MRS HODGE	Here you are, take your tablet.
MR HODGE	Oh, this is the best one yet, this is.
MRS HODGE	Jean was crying.
MR HODGE	So would I be if I was married to him.
MRS HODGE	He can't sue us, can he?
MR HODGE	Don't be stupid, Susan.
MRS HODGE	She asked to speak to you.
MR HODGE	So?
MRS HODGE	She was sobbing and sobbing.
MR HODGE	So what?
MRS HODGE	Why does she always ask to speak to you?
MR HODGE	Don't start this, Susan.
MRS HODGE	I just don't know what you see in her.
MR HODGE	Susan!
MRS HODGE	Such a funny looking thing.
MR HODGE	Susan please . . . I don't feel too well.
MRS HODGE	Here you are then, have another tablet, have twenty.

(*She throws the bottle at him. Lights fade down to black.*)

Scene Seventeen

Loud sirens and flashing lights are fading out across the
stage as the lights come up on the Chapman's. MR CHAPMAN *is*
just slamming the front door.

MRS CHAPMAN   Is that the last of them?

MR CHAPMAN   Who knows!

MRS CHAPMAN   They should arrest him.

MR CHAPMAN   Oh they will eventually, the stupid git. You
              can't waste police time and get away with it.

MRS CHAPMAN   Well he just has — they can't prove it was him.

MR CHAPMAN   I'll get him back for this. They said he's done
              it before so God knows what he got up to with
              the other poor sods that lived here. So are we
              going back to bed or what? I was just getting
              stuck into that.

MRS CHAPMAN   God you're romantic!

MR CHAPMAN   Oh come on Ellen, it's what you want isn't it?

MRS CHAPMAN   Robert I don't think a quick bonk interrupted
              by the local emergency services is what I want
              at all!

MR CHAPMAN   I'll get him back for that, I told you.

MRS CHAPMAN   I don't want you to get him back — I couldn't
              give a shit about him!

MR CHAPMAN   Well you've changed your tune!

MRS CHAPMAN   I just want to know why you want me again all
              of a sudden. Getting him back, sorting him out
              — it's giving you an erection.

MR CHAPMAN   Where the hell did you read that one? The
              sexual therapist's hand book?

MRS CHAPMAN It just didn't feel right that's all. It's not how I want to make love.

MR CHAPMAN So now I can't even do it properly! Jesus Christ, I can't win!

MRS CHAPMAN You're not supposed to WIN! It's not a contest!

MR CHAPMAN It was a figure of speech.

MRS CHAPMAN Do you want to make love to me, Robert?

(*He does not answer.*)

Because if you do I can show you how to —

MR CHAPMAN I know how to.

MRS CHAPMAN Well then . . . let's have another go.

MR CHAPMAN Well I can't now.

MRS CHAPMAN Why not?

MR CHAPMAN Cause it's gone soft.

MRS CHAPMAN Oh, alright then, have your fantasies about Mr Peach — imagine taking him to court or smashing his face in, I don't care just get it back up!

MR CHAPMAN I cannot just get it back up! I'm just an average, ordinary bloke and sometimes Ellen our dicks go soft! I've been trying to keep it up Ellen, all of it, I'm scared to death of not being able to keep it up. I don't know whether I'll keep my job or crash my car or lose my house or be a good role model to a son or abuse a daughter — I don't know anything about myself!

MRS CHAPMAN Hey, hey, it's alright, Robert.

MR CHAPMAN I've worked bloody hard in a boring, overpaid job to bring us to suburbia with you kicking and screaming every inch of the way and once here I even, God forgive me, tried to get on with our neighbours. I've just been doing all the things I was taught to do years before I even met you.

MRS CHAPMAN I know.

MR CHAPMAN If I could run off to a desert island with you and have kids then I'd do it tomorrow but we have to live amongst people, be part of society and I know you'd like to change that society Ellen and I'm not saying you shouldn't but get real — you're not going to manage it, it ain't going to happen!

MRS CHAPMAN So?

MR CHAPMAN So I have to be honest with you and not always think you're getting at me and you have to stop theorising and get into the real world and maybe then we can help each other.

MRS CHAPMAN I'm frightened of the real world.

MR CHAPMAN So am I Ellen, that's why I need you with me.

MRS CHAPMAN Does it mean we have to put up with their behaviour?

MR CHAPMAN No, but it does mean not letting them get to us.

MRS CHAPMAN Ok, Mr Chapman — I'll play it your way for awhile.

MR CHAPMAN That's all I wanted Ellen, a chance.

MRS CHAPMAN It's a deal then?

MR CHAPMAN Deal.

(*They shake on it.*)

Right then Ellen, let's get the bastards!

(*She looks surprised and loud music fills the stage as the lights go to blackout.*)

Scene Eighteen

Music fades out and lights come up on the Hodges on their balcony. It is early morning. MRS HODGE *is dozing.* MR HODGE *is pacing up and down, rubbing his chest. After a little while* MRS HODGE *wakes up.*

MRS HODGE   What are you doing?

MR HODGE   I can't breathe.

MRS HODGE   Sit down — relax.

MR HODGE   I can't, I've got a pain.

MRS HODGE   Shall I call the doctor?

MR HODGE   No, I don't want to see the doctor.

MRS HODGE   Do you want a drink?

MR HODGE   No, I can't breathe.

MRS HODGE   Just relax.

MR HODGE   I've got to get out of here — it's too hot!

MRS HODGE   It's not at all hot — you're just working yourself up.

MR HODGE   I'm going for a walk.

MRS HODGE   Well I'll come with you.

MR HODGE   No! I need some space.

MRS HODGE   Well don't go far Jim, not if you're not feeling well.

MR HODGE   No — right.

            (*He exits.* MRS HODGE *watches him leave. The telephone starts ringing.*)

MRS HODGE   Oh, go away!

(*She throws a cushion at the phone then puts
her hands over her ears.*)

Scene Nineteen

*Lights change to morning at the Peach's. They are in bed —
awake but shattered.*

MRS PEACH   It can't be real.

MR PEACH   What?

MRS PEACH   You can hear her same as me.

MR PEACH   No I can't.

MRS PEACH   If that's real then he must be built like a
               Greek god.

MR PEACH   Chapman?

MRS PEACH   Well you don't think she's got somebody else
               round there, do you?

MR PEACH   She would if she had any sense.

MRS PEACH   She should be so lucky.

MR PEACH   Well Chapman's no Greek god.

MRS PEACH   How do you know?

MR PEACH   I see him all the time.

MRS PEACH   Down there? You see him all the time down
               there?

MR PEACH   What are you talking about? Out there I see
               him — out there all the time — usually when
               he's punching my face in!

MRS PEACH   She's faking it — for me she's faking it — not
               for him — as if I'm interested in her love life!

               (*Short pause.*)

How are you feeling this morning?

MR PEACH   A bit bruised. Have I got a black eye?

MRS PEACH   You'll live.

MR PEACH   No thanks to him. You can take a photograph of me in a minute — I might need it later as evidence.

MRS PEACH   What are you going to do?

MR PEACH   I've told you, haven't I? I'm going to sort it out.

MRS PEACH   Well it can't go on, Harold — not if it's making you unhappy.

MR PEACH   In twenty four years of marriage you have never made me unhappy — not even for a day.

MRS PEACH   Ditto.

MR PEACH   Dotto.

MRS PEACH   Ditto.

MR PEACH   Dotto.

MRS PEACH   Ditto.

MR PEACH   Dotto. Dot.

Scene Twenty

The Chapman's, the same morning. They are laughing hysterically but trying to stifle it as they stand in separate parts of the room. She is making very loud sexual noises and he is banging a shoe on the floor. Then he stands on the sofa and starts jumping up and down as she continues moaning. They improvise around the house trying to make the sex sound as outrageous and loud as they can, banging drawers and pots and pans, etc, for the benefit of their neighbours. Every now and again they come together for a snog and then continue the simulation, collapsing into giggles as the lights fade out.

Scene Twenty One

*Aborigine music as the lights fade up on the Hodges. It is
night.* MRS HODGE *is alone on the balcony, she is looking out
across it, squinting. She picks up a pair of binoculars and
stares through them searchingly. She looks anxious. She sits
down on her chair and picks up a magazine and starts leafing
through it absent-mindedly. She stands up again and peers
over the balcony. Suddenly* MR HODGE *enters. He is drenched
with water.*

MRS HODGE	Oh my God, Jim!
MR HODGE	I went for a swim.
MRS HODGE	In all your clothes?
MR HODGE	A big wave got me — I was only paddling.
MRS HODGE	This isn't Morcambe beach Jim, how often have I told you to be careful of the waves!

(*He is shivering.*)

MR HODGE	I'm freezing.
MRS HODGE	At least it cooled you down, eh?

(*He laughs and shivers at the same time.*)

Here, dry yourself off.

(*She hands him a towel which he covers
himself with like a blanket and sits down.*)

Get those wet clothes off Jim. You can't sit
like, that you'll get pneumonia.

MR HODGE	Sue . . .
MRS HODGE	Yes?
MR HODGE	The sea . . .

MRS HODGE	Yes?
MR HODGE	I don't know what happened.
MRS HODGE	Look, you've had a nasty scare — a shock — you dry yourself and I'll pour you a brandy.
MR HODGE	What time is it?
MRS HODGE	Ten o' clock.
MR HODGE	Did they ring?
MRS HODGE	No, no one rang.
MR HODGE	Only I was looking at the moon and paddling and I heard the telephone ringing — in my head — and the sea looked calm and peaceful and safe and I just kept walking and the phone kept ringing and —
MRS HODGE	I'm having the number changed tomorrow.
MR HODGE	They'll get it somehow.
MRS HODGE	Then I'll get rid of the phone.
MR HODGE	And the letters?
MRS HODGE	We could move house — there are some nice properties further north. Queensland, Ayres Rock!
MR HODGE	They'll find us.
MRS HODGE	They'll tire of us soon Jim, that young couple won't stay there for ever, they'll get people in they like and then they'll tire of us.
MR HODGE	I miss home sometimes.
MRS HODGE	So do I.
MR HODGE	It's so unfair.
MRS HODGE	I know . . . I know.

MR HODGE   I wish we'd never laid eyes on either of them.
                  I was only ever friendly towards them, how
                  was I to know they'd take over our lives like
                  that, to this day if I could get my hands on
                  that estate agent, if I could do it all over
                  again, God Susan, I'd throttle the lot of them!

MRS HODGE   I know . . . I know.

                  (*And the lights fade down.*)

                         Scene Twenty Two

Lights up on the Peach's, who are still in bed. MRS PEACH *has
been dozing. She opens her eyes.*

MRS PEACH   Oh well, best get on.

                  (*She gets out of bed.* MR PEACH *just lies there
                  staring into space. She moves into the sitting
                  area and begins polishing the table with the
                  chip on the foot with great vigour. She opens
                  the little drawer in the end of the table and
                  starts clearing it out to polish the inside.
                  Heaps of papers, mostly bills, have been
                  stuffed into the drawer. She starts collating
                  them into some sort of order. As she does she
                  begins to look confused. She flicks through
                  them as an expression of disbelief forms on
                  her face. She closes her eyes and steadies
                  herself. Then she puts them on the table and
                  starts polishing the inside of the drawer. Her
                  hand seems to touch something unfamiliar.
                  She fumbles around inside the drawer with her
                  hand, slowly pulling out a gun. She holds it in
                  the palm of her hand, staring at it in
                  bewilderment. She feels the weight of it. She
                  passes it from hand to hand. She puts it
                  against her face to feel the cold metal on her
                  cheek. Then she points it in the direction of
                  the bedroom and begins walking extremely
                  slowly towards* MR PEACH. *As she enters the
                  space she stops still and just points it at arm's*

length towards his head. MR PEACH *stares at her expressionless for some time.*)

MR PEACH   Shall I make you a cup of tea?

(*She does not respond.* MR PEACH *gets out of bed and carefully tucks the sheets back in. He puts on his clothes.* MRS PEACH *does not take her eyes or the gun off him. She is very calm.* MR PEACH *walks past her and into the kitchen area.* MRS PEACH *slowly turns and points the gun in the direction of the kitchen. She stands there silently, arm outstretched.* MR PEACH *pops his head round into the sitting area.*)

MR PEACH   It seems we've run out of milk. Shall I go and get some?

(*She does not respond.*)

MR PEACH   Right you are.

(*And he puts on his coat and leaves the house.* MRS PEACH *stands there for a moment, pointing the gun at the front door and then she sits on the sofa and drops it in her lap.*)

                Scene Twenty Three

The lights change to the Hodge's balcony. It is still night. MR HODGE *is lying on the sofa with his eyes closed.* MRS HODGE *enters from another part of the house.*

MRS HODGE   I thought we could go on a little trip tomorrow Jim, maybe take the car and drive up to the Blue Mountains. Have a picnic, even stay over night. I'll ring Anthony and see if he wants to come. A proper family outing, take advantage of our situation, do all the things we said we'd do before we came out here. A change of attitude, that's all we need, eh?

(*He does not respond.*)

Whadda ya say, sport? A bush walk, the
theatre, cinema, or throw a party — we have
kept ourselves to ourselves — maybe it's time
— maybe we could face it now — they really
do seem nice next door — we can't tar
everybody with the same brush — not forever
. . . Jim!

(*She is irritated.*)

Ah, come on Jim, snap out of it! You've got to
pull yourself together, we both have. The past
is the past, we've got to keep it there. Ok?
Jim? . . . Jim! . . . Jim! . . . Jim . . .

(*She sits beside him and shakes him. His body
is lifeless.*)

Oh, Jim.

(*She just holds his hand and kisses it as the
lights fade down to black.*)

Scene Twenty Four

Lights come back up on the Peach's. MR PEACH *has just
entered with a bottle of milk. He notices that* MRS PEACH *is no
longer holding the gun. She hears him enter.*

MRS PEACH	It said that they're going to take the house off us.
MR PEACH	I know what it said Jean, but just because it said it, doesn't make it true.
MRS PEACH	But why does it say that, Harold?
MR PEACH	Because it does Jean, you know, that's what they do to hard-working decent folk in this country now. Years ago a snotty little graduate in nappies wouldn't have sent you an anonymous threatening letter because you forgot — FORGOT, Jean, to make a few

payments on your mortgage. They used to have respect, the banks and building societies, they used to look after the likes of me but not now, oh no — now they tread on you like a piece of dirt, an insect under foot — splat!

MRS PEACH   Well if you only forgot to pay the mortgage Harold, why don't you explain that to them? I'm sure they'll understand, I mean you'll pay back the bits you missed, won't you?

MR PEACH   I already have paid it back Jean, so don't you worry your head — ssssh, sssssh, there is nothing, nothing to worry about. You lie here on my chest, I like to feel your hair. You always did have lovely hair, when you were a girl all the boys talked about it.

MRS PEACH   Did they?

MR PEACH   Oh yes, they all wanted you Jean, with your shiny golden hair and who did you choose out of every boy in the area?

MRS PEACH   You, Harold.

MR PEACH   Me Jean, you chose me. And we've done alright for ourselves, you and me, we've kept the wolves and monsters from our door, we've created a little paradise for ourselves here and nobody is going to ever take that away from us because we haven't robbed it, we haven't blackmailed or threatened anyone to get it, no Jean, we've earned it.

(MRS PEACH *digests the information for a moment.*)

MRS PEACH   I spy with my little eye, something beginning with . . .

(*She looks around the room — there is only one piece of furniture left.*)

. . . T.

MR PEACH   Table?

MRS PEACH   Yes!

                  (*And she smiles as* MR PEACH *takes the gun
                  from her lap and holds it as the lights fade
                  down to black.*)

                        Scene Twenty Five

*The Chapman's. They are still in bed but both are sharing a
cigarette. They look serenely happy and* MR CHAPMAN *tickles
his wife playfully.*

MRS CHAPMAN   Get off me!

MR CHAPMAN   Incey-wincey spider, climbed up the spout,
                 along came the rain and washed the spider
                 out, out came the sunshine and dried up all
                 the rain, then incey-wincey spider went
                 climbing up again.

MRS CHAPMAN   You naughty, naughty spider, give — me — a
                 — kiss!

                 (*They kiss and cuddle as* MR PEACH *suddenly
                 walks into the room. They look up in
                 amazement.*)

MR CHAPMAN   What the. . . ?! How the hell did you get in?!!

MR PEACH   Spare key under the mat, Mr Chapman.

MR CHAPMAN   GET OUT!

MR PEACH   Why should I?

MR CHAPMAN   What do you want Peach?

MR PEACH   Shut up!

MR CHAPMAN   Get out before I call the police!

MR PEACH	I've already called them — they're on their way.
MR CHAPMAN	I SAID GET OUT!
	(MR CHAPMAN *gets out of bed.* MR PEACH *produces a gun, stopping* CHAPMAN *in his tracks. Silence.*)
MRS CHAPMAN	It is Harold, isn't it?
MR PEACH	That's right, yes.
MRS CHAPMAN	Alright then, Harold — put it down.
MR PEACH	I said shut up!
MR CHAPMAN	Christ, Peach — I'm sorry about the pansies — I've been under a lot of pressure — I was drunk — I never meant to hit you.
MR PEACH	Oh, but you did hit me Mr Chapman.
MR CHAPMAN	Please God, I never meant to . . .
MRS CHAPMAN	Listen Harold, what do you want?
MR PEACH	Don't you talk to me like that.
MR CHAPMAN	Leave her out of this.
MR PEACH	She's just as involved as you are — with your nice cars and your nice wife leading me up the garden path, taking her clothes off in public, it's not decent.
MR CHAPMAN	You like the car — you can have the car.
MR PEACH	I don't like sunroofs actually, Chapman.
MR CHAPMAN	Then what the hell do you want?
MR PEACH	I want to see you on your knees — both of you, kneel down.
MRS CHAPMAN	Fuck off!

MR CHAPMAN   Do it Ellen!

MR PEACH   Yes, do it Ellen — quick!

MRS CHAPMAN   If you want to talk — I can help you — but
                  I'm not doing anything else.

MR CHAPMAN   For God's sake, Ellen!

MRS CHAPMAN   Do you want to talk, Harold?

                  (MR PEACH *suddenly climbs into bed with* MRS
                  CHAPMAN.)

MR CHAPMAN   What the hell do you think you're playing
                  at?!!!

MRS CHAPMAN   It's alright, Robert — he just wants to talk,
                  don't you Harold?

                  (MR PEACH *points the gun at* MR CHAPMAN.)

MR PEACH   That's right Chapman, I just want to spend
                  some time with your wife.

MR CHAPMAN   Ellen — let me deal with this — we have a
                  deal remember!

MRS CHAPMAN   Shut up, Robert!

MR PEACH   Yes, shut up Robert!

                  (MR PEACH *turns his head to* MRS CHAPMAN *but
                  keeps pointing the gun at* MR CHAPMAN. *He
                  speaks in a hushed and dangerously intimate
                  voice.*)

MR PEACH   Hello Ellen. It is Ellen, isn't it?

MRS CHAPMAN   Yes.

MR PEACH   Well then Ellen, isn't this cosy?

MRS CHAPMAN   I can help you, you know, Harold.

MR PEACH   Can you really? And how do you propose to do that?

MRS CHAPMAN   First of all I think you should consider what you hope to achieve by all this.

MR PEACH   Right you are . . . I've considered it.

MRS CHAPMAN   Would you like to share that with me?

MR PEACH   You really are a flirt, aren't you Ellen?

MRS CHAPMAN   I think you're projecting your fantasy onto me Mr Peach, I don't consider myself to be flirting.

MR PEACH   So you take your top off for all the boys, do you?

MRS CHAPMAN   I simply do what I like in my own garden.

MR PEACH   How lucky you are, to be able to do just what you like.

MRS CHAPMAN   Am I? If this is how I pay for it . . .

MR PEACH   We all have to pay for it Ellen and we pay for it always when we least expect it, for when they come, they come with smiles, don't they? Carrying knives and guns and hatchets. In the dead of night they come, silently, with great stealth. You think you can smell them but it's your own stench and sweat and shit, you try and move but you are locked in position, you try and scream but nothing, you frantically, foolishly rack your brain to think — come on, think! — of some way to defend yourself to be ready for them when they come because they surely will come and when they do they'll get you and there's not a damned thing you can do about it.

MRS CHAPMAN   And who are "they", Harold?

MR PEACH   That's the point isn't it? They don't tell you,
                and when they've taken everything away from
                you — there is only you left to take.

MRS CHAPMAN   And where do you think they will take you,
                Harold?

MR PEACH   To a dark place with no windows, that's where
                they'll take me.

MR CHAPMAN   Come on Harold, put the gun down.

MR PEACH   It's Mr Peach to you!!!

                (*And he makes a sudden aggressive movement
                with the gun in the direction of* MR CHAPMAN'S
                head as he turns to look at him.)

MR CHAPMAN   OK, Peach — OK!

                (MR PEACH *continues to* MRS CHAPMAN.)

MR PEACH   You know I always wanted to go to Australia,
                me and Jean often talked about it — getting
                out of the rat race. I hear it's beautiful this
                time of year. You ever been to Australia, Mr
                Chapman?

MR CHAPMAN   Yes, we went for our honeymoon.

MR PEACH   And how did you like it?

MR CHAPMAN   (*mutters*) Fine.

MR PEACH   What?

MR CHAPMAN   I said fine.

MR PEACH   Yes, I'm sure you did. You know this really is
                a nice house.

MR CHAPMAN   Ellen doesn't like it — do you Ellen?

MR PEACH   Don't you Ellen? Bit ordinary for you I
                suppose, you having been to Australia. You
                know me and Jean have always admired this
                house — Jean more than me really, she's had
                her eye on it for some time — she'd like this
                room, the way you've done it out.

MRS CHAPMAN   Harold, what do you want?

MR PEACH   Not nearly as much as you'd think.

                (MR CHAPMAN *suddenly screams out and goes
                to dive on* MR PEACH, MRS CHAPMAN *screams
                "No!", but* MR PEACH *has shot him in the
                shoulder.* MR CHAPMAN *writhes about the floor,
                moaning in agony. The loud sound of sirens
                and flashing lights approaching floods the
                stage.* MR PEACH *waves the gun dangerously.
                Suddenly* MRS PEACH *bursts into the bedroom
                and speaks very urgently.*)

MRS PEACH   Look Harold, I'm not a fool, you're in some
                kind of trouble, aren't you? You couldn't have
                just forgotten to pay the bills, there's
                something more going on. Are you having
                trouble at work? And who were those man at
                the door and why can't things be like they
                used to be when things were peaceful and we
                had nice neighbours and why don't we go on
                holiday any more and I love those wardrobes,
                why can't I have wardrobes like that?

                (*Everyone just stares at* MRS PEACH *and she
                stares back at them, slightly bemused by what
                she now sees in front of her.* MR PEACH
                *screams and the lights snap to black just
                before the gun goes off again. Loud exciting
                music fills the theatre.*)